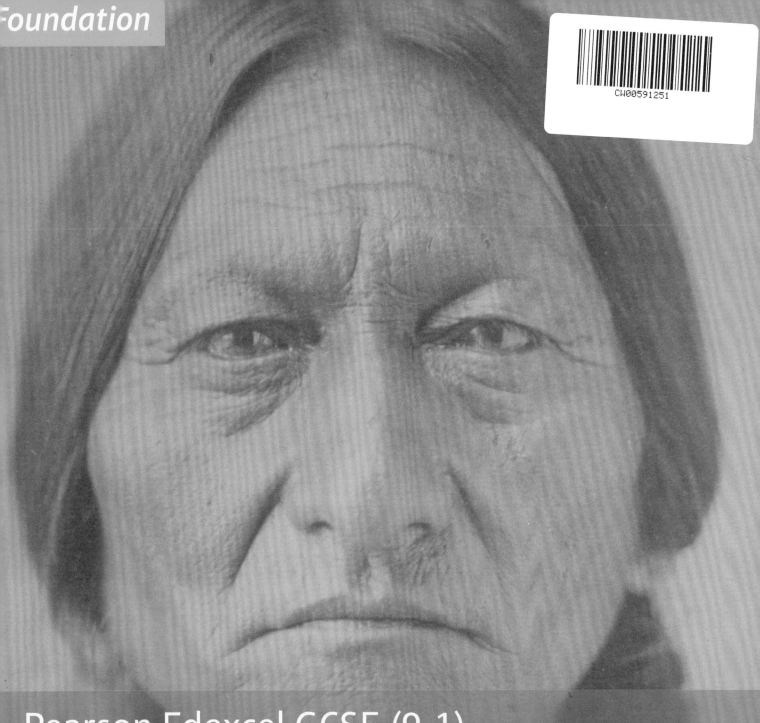

Foundation

Pearson Edexcel GCSE (9-1)

History

The American West, c1835–c1895

Series Editor: Angela Leonard   Author: Rob Bircher

Pearson

Published by Pearson Education Limited, 80 Strand, London, WC2R 0RL.

www.pearsonschoolsandfecolleges.co.uk

Copies of official specifications for all Edexcel qualifications may be found on the website: www.edexcel.com

Text © Pearson Education Limited 2018

Series editor: Angela Leonard
Designed by Colin Tilley Loughrey, Pearson Education Limited
Typeset by QBS Learning
Original illustrations © Pearson Education Limited
Illustrated by KJA Artists Illustration Agency and Phoenix Photosetting, Chatham, Kent and QBS Learning.

Cover design by Colin Tilley Loughrey
Cover photo © Bridgeman Art Library Ltd: Private Collection

The right of Rob Bircher to be identified as author of this work has been asserted by him in accordance with the Copyright, Designs and Patents Act 1988.

First published 2018

21 20 19 18
10 9 8 7 6 5 4 3 2 1

British Library Cataloguing in Publication Data
A catalogue record for this book is available from the British Library.
ISBN 978 1 292 25830 0

Printed in Slovakia by Neografia

A note from the publisher
1. While the publishers have made every attempt to ensure that advice on the qualification and its assessment is accurate, the official specification and associated assessment guidance materials are the only authoritative source of information and should always be referred to for definitive guidance.

Pearson examiners have not contributed to any sections in this resource relevant to examination papers for which they have responsibility.

2. Pearson has robust editorial processes, including answer and fact checks, to ensure the accuracy of the content in this publication, and every effort is made to ensure this publication is free of errors. We are, however, only human, and occasionally errors do occur. Pearson is not liable for any misunderstandings that arise as a result of errors in this publication, but it is our priority to ensure that the content is accurate. If you spot an error, please do contact us at resourcescorrections@pearson.com so we can make sure it is corrected.

Websites
Pearson Education Limited is not responsible for the content of any external internet sites. It is essential for tutors to preview each website before using it in class so as to ensure that the URL is still accurate, relevant and appropriate. We suggest that tutors bookmark useful websites and consider enabling students to access them through the school/college intranet.

Contents

What's covered?

This book covers The American West, c1835-c1895. This unit makes up 20% of your GCSE course, and will be examined in Paper 2.

Period studies cover a specific period of time of around 50 years, and require you to know about and be able to analyse the events surrounding important developments and issues that happened in this period. You need to understand how the different topics covered fit into the overall narrative. This book also explains the different types of exam questions you will need to answer, and includes advice and example answers to help you improve.

Features

As well as a clear, detailed explanation of the key knowledge you will need, you will also find a number of features in the book:

Key terms

Where you see a word followed by an asterisk, like this: Frontier*, you will be able to find a Key Terms box on that page that explains what the word means.

> **Key term**
>
> **Frontier***
> The border between two countries, or the border between a 'civilised' country and undeveloped areas.

Activities

Every few pages, you'll find a box containing some activities designed to help check and embed knowledge and get you to really think about what you've studied. The activities start simple, but might get more challenging as you work through them.

Summaries and Checkpoints

At the end of each chunk of learning, the main points are summarised in a series of bullet points – great for embedding the core knowledge, and handy for revision.

Checkpoints help you to check and reflect on your learning. The Strengthen section helps you to consolidate knowledge and understanding, and check that you've grasped the basic ideas and skills. The Challenge questions push you to go beyond just

understanding the information, and into evaluation and analysis of what you've studied.

Sources and Interpretations

Although source work and interpretations do not appear in Paper 2, you'll still find interesting contemporary material throughout the books, showing what people from the period said, thought or created, helping you to build your understanding of people in the past.

The book also includes extracts from the work of historians, showing how experts have interpreted the events you've been studying.

> **Source C**
>
> A photo showing Pinkerton agents. The man sitting down is the son of Alfred Pinkerton, who founded Pinkerton's National Detective Agency in 1850.
>
>

> **Interpretation 1**
>
> From *The Great American Desert* (1966) by W. E. Hollon. Here he describes how the right conditions came about to cause the rapid growth of the cattle industry.
>
> Suddenly, the right conditions fell into place... the Civil War brought an increased demand for beef... settlers learned that cattle could thrive on the native grass and survive the drastic changes in climate; the transcontinental railroads pushed to the Pacific... .

Extend your knowledge

These features contain useful additional information that adds depth to your knowledge, and to your answers. The information is closely related to the key issues in the unit, and questions are sometimes included, helping you to link the new details to the main content.

> **Extend your knowledge**
>
> **Crossing Indian Territory**
>
> The Chisholm Trail went through Indian Territory, the land (now Oklahoma) that had been granted to the eastern tribes of American Indians moved west by the Indian Removal Act (see page 16). These tribes required payment from the cowboys in return for permission to cross their lands. Warriors patrolled the lands to make sure payments were collected. Conflicts sometimes occurred when trail bosses refused to pay.

Exam-style questions and tips

The book also includes extra exam-style questions you can use to practise. These appear in the chapters and are accompanied by a tip to help you get started on an answer.

> **Exam-style question, Section A**
>
> Write a narrative account analysing the ways in which the US government policy towards the Plains Indians developed in the period 1835–51.
>
> You may use the following in your answer:
> - the Permanent Indian Frontier (c1834)
> - the Indian Appropriations Act (1851)
>
> You **must** also use information of your own. **8 marks**

> **Exam tip**
>
> Plan your answer first by listing the main developments of 1835–51 in sequence. This will help you structure your answer and think about how one event links to the next.

Recap pages

At the end of each chapter, you'll find a page designed to help you to consolidate and reflect on the chapter as a whole. Each recap page includes a recall quiz, ideal for quickly checking your knowledge or for revision. Recap pages also include activities designed to help you summarise and analyse what you've learned, and also reflect on how each chapter links to other parts of the unit.

THINKING HISTORICALLY

These activities are designed to help you develop a better understanding of how history is constructed, and are focused on the key areas of Evidence, Interpretations, Cause & Consequence and Change & Continuity. In the Period Study, you will come across an activity on Cause & Consequence, as this is a key focus for this unit.

The Thinking Historically approach has been developed in conjunction with Dr Arthur Chapman and the Institute of Education, UCL. It is based on research into the misconceptions that can hold students back in history.

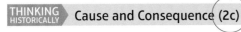 **THINKING HISTORICALLY** Cause and Consequence **(2c)** — conceptual map reference

The Thinking Historically conceptual map can be found at: www.pearsonschools.co.uk/thinkinghistoricallygcse

WRITING HISTORICALLY

At the end of most chapters is a spread dedicated to helping you improve your writing skills. These include simple techniques you can use in your writing to make your answers clearer, more precise and better focused on the question you're answering.

The Writing Historically approach is based on the *Grammar for Writing* pedagogy developed by a team at the University of Exeter and popular in many English departments. Each spread uses examples from the preceding chapter, so it's relevant to what you've just been studying.

Preparing for your exams

At the back of the book, you'll find a special section dedicated to explaining and exemplifying the new Edexcel GCSE History exams. Advice on the demands of this paper, written by Angela Leonard, helps you prepare for and approach the exam with confidence. Each question type is explained through annotated sample answers at two levels, showing clearly how answers can be improved.

Pearson Progression Scale: This icon indicates the Step that a sample answer has been graded at on the Pearson Progression Scale.

> *This book is also available as an online ActiveBook, which can be licensed for your whole institution.*

Settling the Plains

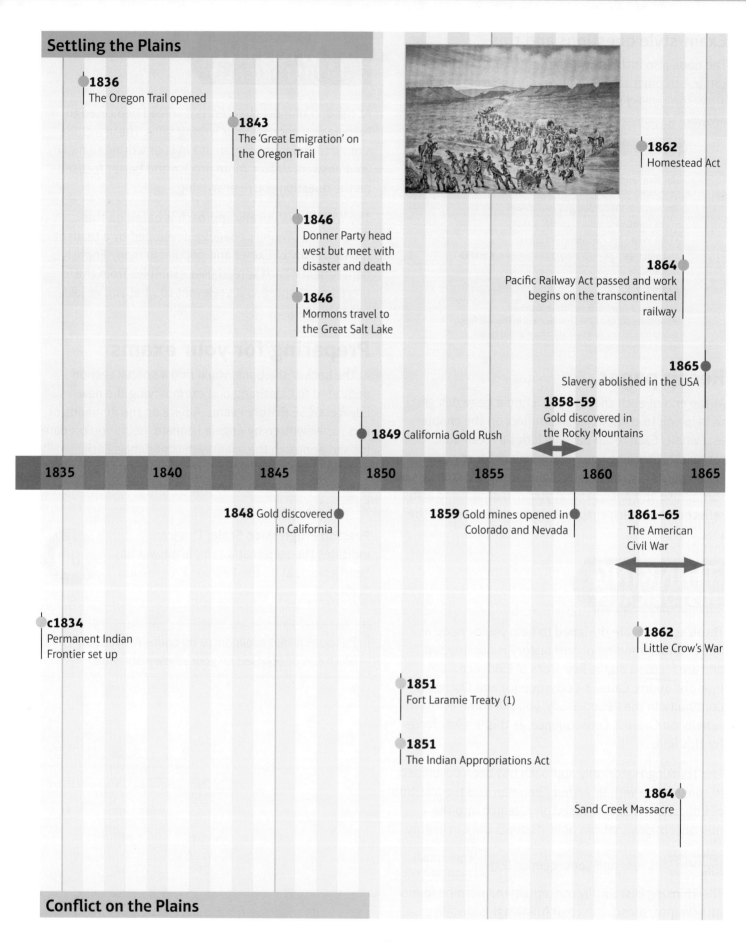

1836
The Oregon Trail opened

1843
The 'Great Emigration' on the Oregon Trail

1846
Donner Party head west but meet with disaster and death

1846
Mormons travel to the Great Salt Lake

1849 California Gold Rush

1862
Homestead Act

1864
Pacific Railway Act passed and work begins on the transcontinental railway

1865
Slavery abolished in the USA

1858–59
Gold discovered in the Rocky Mountains

1835	1840	1845	1850	1855	1860	1865

1848 Gold discovered in California

1859 Gold mines opened in Colorado and Nevada

1861–65
The American Civil War

c1834
Permanent Indian Frontier set up

1862
Little Crow's War

1851
Fort Laramie Treaty (1)

1851
The Indian Appropriations Act

1864
Sand Creek Massacre

Conflict on the Plains

1866
Goodnight and Loving reach Fort Sumner with a herd of cattle

1867
Abilene becomes the first cow town

1869
First Transcontinental Railroad completed

1870
Cattle Ranching begins on the Plains, leading to the 'Open Range'

1873
Timber Culture Act

1874
Barbed wire begins to be mass-produced

1874
Wind-powered water pump introduced

1879
Exoduster Movement

1881
The OK Corral

1886–87
Severe winter leads to the end of the open range

1892
Johnson County War

1893
Oklahoma Land Rush

1870	1875	1880	1885	1890	1895

1866
Fetterman's Trap

1866–68
Red Cloud's War

1874
Custer leads expedition to the Black Hills

1885
All Plains Indians are resettled on to reservations

1868
'The Winter Campaign'

1876–81
The Great Sioux War

1887
Dawes Act

1868
President Grant's 'Peace Policy'

1890
Wounded Knee Massacre

1868
Fort Laramie Treaty (2)

1876
The Battle of the Little Big Horn

1890
The US government closes Frontier

01 | The early settlement of the West, c1835–c1862

The American West is the land making up two-thirds of the USA that is west of the Mississippi River. The Great Plains makes up a lot of the American West. In the early 19th century, white Americans called the Plains 'The Great American Desert'. They were happy to leave it to the American Indians (sometimes called Native Americans). At that time, white Americans lived in the east of America.

By the 1840s, new developments brought changes in the east and west of America that 'pushed' and 'pulled' people to move west to Oregon and California and encouraged them to make a living farming the Plains. The growing number of settlers moving across the Plains caused problems between settlers and Plains Indians.

Mass migration to the West, following the California Gold Rush, also caused major problems. This was because there was not enough law enforcement. As a result, mining towns tried to enforce the law themselves, but this did not solve the problem.

Learning outcomes

By the end of this chapter, you will:

- understand the way of life and beliefs of the Plains Indians
- understand why white Americans migrated westwards and why this migration was challenging
- understand why conflict and tension developed between different groups of people in the West.

1.1 The Plains Indians: their beliefs and way of life

Learning outcomes

- Understand the ways of life of the Plains Indians.
- Understand the Plains Indians' beliefs about land and nature, and their attitudes to war and property.
- Understand the US government support for westward expansion and the significance of the Permanent Indian Frontier (c1834) and the Indian Appropriations Act (1851).

Who were the Plains Indians?

Many different American Indian tribes made up the people known as the Plains Indians. Figure 1.1 shows some of the main Plains Indian tribes and where they lived on the Great Plains.

Plains Indian society

Each tribe was made up of different bands. Bands* could be several hundred people or just 20 or 30 people. In order to survive, the different bands within a tribe worked together. All the different bands in a tribe usually met in the summer for a great tribal camp. As well as being social and religious occasions, these were times when a tribe could co-operate to make sure they survived on the Plains.

The Sioux nation* was made up of the Lakota, Dakota and Nakota tribes. In turn, the Lakota was made up of seven smaller tribes. Two of these were called the Oglala and Hunkpapa.

Key terms

Bands*
Sometimes several different bands made up a tribe.

Nation*
Some Plains Indian tribes, such as a the Sioux, were so large that they were known as nations. A nation was made up of several tribes.

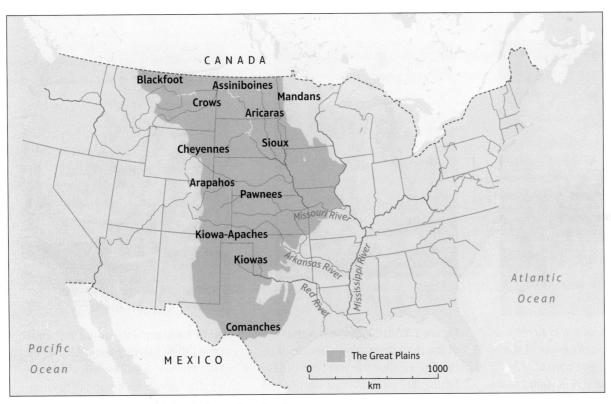

Figure 1.1 Where the main Plains Indian tribes lived.

Chiefs and councils

Chiefs were the leaders of the Plains Indians. They were always men. Each tribe could have many chiefs: a war chief, a spiritual chief and a chief who led negotiations with other tribes. White Americans* found this difficult to understand. They were used to having just one leader.

- There was no one way of choosing a chief. Chiefs were chosen because of their wisdom, leadership or for their skill as warriors or hunters. Chiefs were rarely chiefs for life.

- Each band had a band chief, who was chosen to guide the band, for example in finding food.

- Band chiefs and elders* made up the tribe's council. In some tribes, the council could decide to go to war against another tribe, or discuss a peace treaty.

- Everyone could give their opinion in the council. No decision was made until everyone had agreed to it.

- In tribes like the Lakota Sioux, chiefs had no power to tell their people what to do. Bands made their own decisions.

Famous chiefs

Some chiefs became famous because of their leadership in wars against white Americans.

For example, **Red Cloud** (see Figure 1.2) was a Lakota Sioux chief who brought together Sioux and Cheyenne tribes in 'Red Cloud's War' against white Americans (see page 66). The war forced the US government to pull the army out of Sioux lands, in return for peace.

However, many Sioux followed a chief called **Sitting Bull** (see Figure 1.3), who rejected the peace treaty, and a chief called **Crazy Horse** (see Figure 1.4).

Key terms
White Americans* Immigrants from Europe and their descendants.
Elders* Older members of the band.
c1822* The c before this date stands for 'circa', which means around. A c used like this shows that historians are not certain about a date.

Figure 1.2 Red Cloud was a chief of the Oglala Lakota people of the Sioux nation. He was born c1822* and became a very important Lakota war leader.

Figure 1.3 Sitting Bull was a chief of the Hunkpapa Lakota people of the Sioux nation. He was born c1831. Sitting Bull was a famous warrior and holy man.

Figure 1.4 Crazy Horse was a war leader of the Oglala Lakota people. He was born c1842 and was a well-known warrior. He was also famous for his ability to enter the spirit world through visions.

Warrior brotherhoods

Plains Indians also had warrior **brotherhoods**. There were several different brotherhoods within a tribe. Young men joined after showing their bravery and skill in fighting with other tribes.

- Warrior brotherhoods trained young men in fighting skills. They also taught young men about the tribe's beliefs and values.
- In many Plains Indian tribes, warrior brotherhoods did not have to do what their tribe's council said. They did not always respect peace treaties that the council had agreed to.
- Leading men from the brotherhoods were invited to join a guard unit for the whole tribe. This guard unit organised the tribe's yearly buffalo hunt, made sure old and ill tribe members were fed, and chose where the tribe should make camp.

Women and Plains Indian society

Women could not be chiefs. A successful man could have more than one wife. This sounds as if women were not valued in Plains Indian society. In fact, they had important roles and were respected very highly. Both men and women had set roles that could not change. Both needed to perform their role with great skill if the tribe was to survive.

Activity ?

The US government could not understand why, when they agreed a treaty with the chief of the tribe, many of the Plains Indians then failed to follow the agreements set out in the treaty. Use the information on pages 10 and 11 to write a short explanation for this behaviour.

Use the following sentence starters in your answer:

'In tribes like the Lakota Sioux, chiefs had no power to command…'

'If a chief signed a treaty with the US government, this did not mean that the rest of the tribe would…'

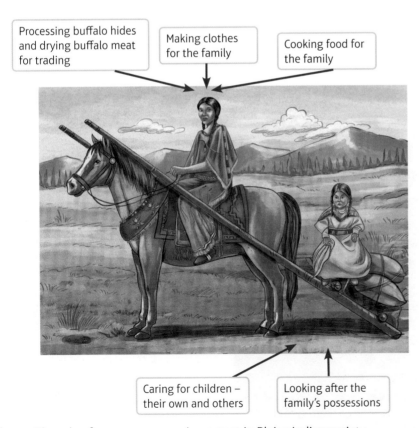

Processing buffalo hides and drying buffalo meat for trading

Making clothes for the family

Cooking food for the family

Caring for children – their own and others

Looking after the family's possessions

Figure: The role of women was very important in Plains Indian society.

Survival on the Great Plains

The Great Plains have hot summers and very cold winters. The Plains are also very dry, with few streams or rivers. When rain comes, it is often in thunderstorms. Lightning flashes sometimes cause fires that sweep across the Plains, burning the dry grass and anything else caught in their way.

Survival for the Plains Indians depended on hunting buffalo on horseback. Huge herds of buffalo moved across the Plains looking for fresh grass. The Plains Indians followed the buffalo through the summer and autumn. Plains Indians had developed:

- amazing horse-riding and archery skills, so they could hunt the buffalo
- a travelling (nomadic*) lifestyle: tipis* which could be easily put up and taken down and travois* to carry each family's belongings to their next camp
- skills to use every part of the buffalo for food, fuel (buffalo dung), clothing, shelter, ornaments, gifts and toys. Buffalo meat was preserved by drying it in the sun.
- great respect for the buffalo. Plains Indians believed that all nature and the land itself must be treated with great respect. Otherwise the spirits that lived in everything would no longer help the Plains Indians survive.

In the harsh winters of the Great Plains, most tribes moved into lodges. These were circular buildings made of earth and wooden logs.

Extend your knowledge

Beliefs about the buffalo

The one part of the buffalo that Plains Indians did not use was the heart. The heart was cut from the dead animal and left on the Plains. Plains Indians believed this gave new life to the herd.

Key terms

Nomadic*

When people move with all their belongings and animals from place to place.

Tipis*

Tent-like homes made of animal hide stretched over wooden poles. The pyramid shape of the tipi could stand up to strong winds.

Travois*

A framework on which Plains Indians carried their belongings. It was pulled by a dog or horse.

Source A

A painting by Charles Marion Russell showing Plains Indians hunting a herd of buffalo across the Great Plains. It was painted in 1887.

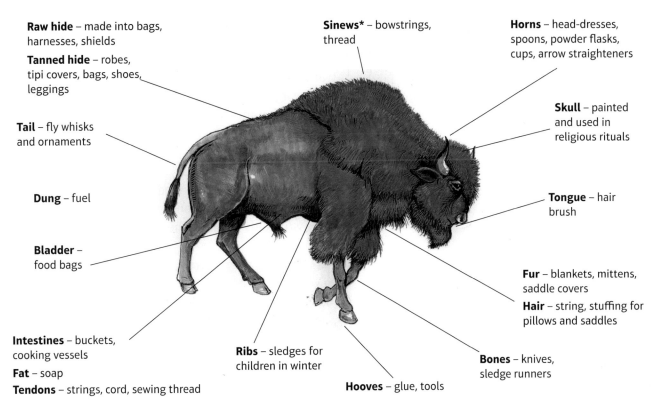

Raw hide – made into bags, harnesses, shields

Tanned hide – robes, tipi covers, bags, shoes, leggings

Tail – fly whisks and ornaments

Dung – fuel

Bladder – food bags

Intestines – buckets, cooking vessels

Fat – soap

Tendons – strings, cord, sewing thread

Sinews* – bowstrings, thread

Ribs – sledges for children in winter

Hooves – glue, tools

Horns – head-dresses, spoons, powder flasks, cups, arrow straighteners

Skull – painted and used in religious rituals

Tongue – hair brush

Fur – blankets, mittens, saddle covers

Hair – string, stuffing for pillows and saddles

Bones – knives, sledge runners

Figure 1.5 The uses of the buffalo.

The importance of horses to Plains Indians

Plains Indians needed horses to hunt buffalo and to travel across the Plains in the search for food. Raids on other tribes or white settlers* were often to steal horses. In the 1870s, the 2,900 Hunkpapa Sioux had 3,500 horses.

Key terms
Sinews*
Tough pieces of string-like body tissue that joins muscles to bones.
Settlers*
People who move into an area to live there.

Beliefs about nature and land
Beliefs about nature

Everything in nature has a spirit. These spirits could choose to help people or harm people.

It was very important to respect the spirits in nature. Plains Indians never tried to control nature or change nature in the way that white Americans did.

It was possible to contact the spirit world through visions and special dances. For example, Plains Indians would dance so that the spirits would help them find buffalo to hunt.

Figure: Plains Indians' beliefs about nature.

Activities	?

1 Describe two ways of life that helped the Plains Indians survive on the Great Plains.

2 Chiefs were chosen for their special skills. Work in groups to choose three chiefs with three different skills, such as: a chief who remembers what the homework was, a humour chief, or a chief who gives sensible advice. Make a list of the advantages and disadvantages of being one of the three chiefs you have chosen.

3 White Americans lived in the same place and went to work each day in the same place. Describe three differences between the life of a white American and a Plains Indian.

Beliefs about land

- Indians did not own land in the way that white Americans did. Families in some tribes might own small garden areas. But no one Indian owned the land they all used for hunting. Land could not be bought or sold in Plains Indian society.

- Plains Indians had sacred* areas. These were often linked to the history of their tribe. For example, what white Americans called the Black Hills of South Dakota were sacred to the Lakota Sioux. They called this area Paha Sapa and believed it was where their tribe came from.

Attitudes to war

- Life on the Plains was very tough, so tribes fought each other often over resources. For example, bands would raid other tribes to steal horses or women and children.

- Braves (warriors) were very important for the tribe's survival. They were often the best hunters and guarded the tribe as well.

As a result, Plains Indian society tried to limit the number of people who got killed or maimed (badly wounded) in fights.

- One way was to run away if a raid started to turn into a fight.

- Another was a special type of fighting called '**counting coup**'. This meant hitting another brave with a blow (rather than trying to kill them), and getting away before the other brave could hit you back.

Interpretation 1

From *The Cheyennes* (1978) by E. A. Hoebel.

War was transformed into a great game in which scoring against the enemy often took precedence [more importance] over killing him. The scoring was in the counting coup – touching or striking an enemy with hand or weapons. Coups counted within an enemy encampment [camp] ranked the highest of all. A man's rank as a warrior depended on two factors: his total 'score' in coups, and his ability to lead successful raids in which Cheyenne losses were low.

Activity

Plains Indians' beliefs about land and nature and war and fighting had an impact on relations between Plains Indian tribes and white settlers. Using what you know, explain what you think Plains Indian attitudes towards the following situations would have been. Discuss each situation in pairs.

a White settlers fence off land that the tribe uses for hunting and then plough it for crops.

b White people start mining for gold in the Black Hills area of South Dakota.

c The US government tells the chiefs of the tribal council that the warrior brotherhoods must stay away from white people travelling through the tribe's hunting lands.

d The US government demands that Plains Indian teenagers should go to school in white cities and learn about Christianity.

Key term

Sacred*

Very important or greatly respected, often because of religious beliefs.

The US government policy towards the Plains Indians

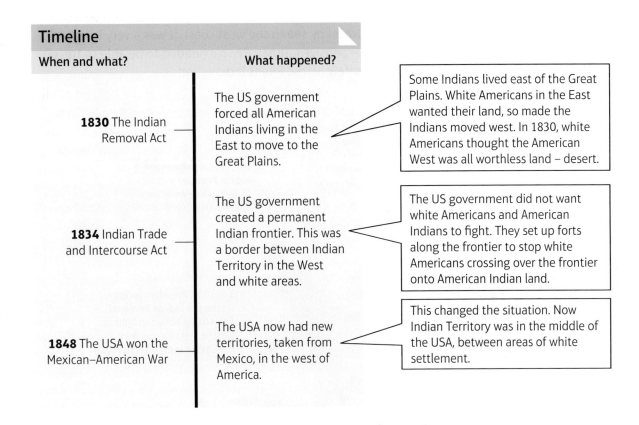

Timeline

When and what?	What happened?	
1830 The Indian Removal Act	The US government forced all American Indians living in the East to move to the Great Plains.	Some Indians lived east of the Great Plains. White Americans in the East wanted their land, so made the Indians moved west. In 1830, white Americans thought the American West was all worthless land – desert.
1834 Indian Trade and Intercourse Act	The US government created a permanent Indian frontier. This was a border between Indian Territory in the West and white areas.	The US government did not want white Americans and American Indians to fight. They set up forts along the frontier to stop white Americans crossing over the frontier onto American Indian land.
1848 The USA won the Mexican–American War	The USA now had new territories, taken from Mexico, in the west of America.	This changed the situation. Now Indian Territory was in the middle of the USA, between areas of white settlement.

Conflicts over land

- Most white Americans thought that American Indians were savages*. They thought it was right to take land away from them if white people needed it.
- This was because white Americans thought they were making the land better by using it to grow crops, or dig up gold and silver from it, or cut down its trees for timber. They thought Indians did not develop the land they used.
- This led to conflict because white Americans tried to force American Indians off their land.

All through the 19th century, the US federal* government tried to sort out 'the Indian problem' as the number of white Americans in the West grew and conflict between white Americans and Plains Indians over land increased.

The US government tackled this conflict in two ways:

- by keeping white settlers and Plains Indians apart
- by encouraging Plains Indians to become like white settlers.

Key terms

Savages*
Not civilised people.

Federal*
The USA is a union of states. Each state has its own state government. The federal government governs over all the states.

A 'permanent' Indian Frontier* and westward expansion

> ### Key term
>
> **Frontier***
>
> The border between two countries, or the border between a 'civilised' country and undeveloped areas.

Government support for westward expansion

The US government wanted US citizens to move into its new territories in the West. Although settlers could travel by sea to the west coast, it was a very long and expensive journey. People needed to be able to travel safely across Plains Indians' lands.

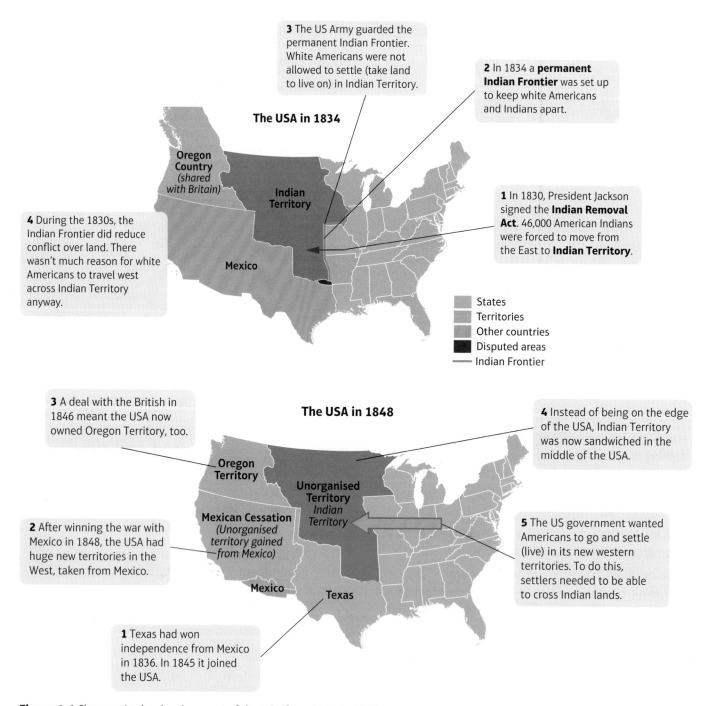

3 The US Army guarded the permanent Indian Frontier. White Americans were not allowed to settle (take land to live on) in Indian Territory.

2 In 1834 a **permanent Indian Frontier** was set up to keep white Americans and Indians apart.

The USA in 1834

1 In 1830, President Jackson signed the **Indian Removal Act**. 46,000 American Indians were forced to move from the East to **Indian Territory**.

4 During the 1830s, the Indian Frontier did reduce conflict over land. There wasn't much reason for white Americans to travel west across Indian Territory anyway.

States
Territories
Other countries
Disputed areas
— Indian Frontier

3 A deal with the British in 1846 meant the USA now owned Oregon Territory, too.

The USA in 1848

4 Instead of being on the edge of the USA, Indian Territory was now sandwiched in the middle of the USA.

2 After winning the war with Mexico in 1848, the USA had huge new territories in the West, taken from Mexico.

5 The US government wanted Americans to go and settle (live) in its new western territories. To do this, settlers needed to be able to cross Indian lands.

1 Texas had won independence from Mexico in 1836. In 1845 it joined the USA.

Figure 1.6 Changes in the development of the USA from 1834 to 1848.

The Indian Appropriations Act (1851)

By reducing the amount of land that Plains Indians had available for hunting, the government hoped to encourage them to take up farming. The idea was that once Plains Indians became farmers, they could begin to live like white Americans. This policy led to the Indian Appropriations Act in 1851.

> People travelling to the West used trails* to cross Indian land. They were worried about American Indians attacking them.

↓

> The US government used the Army to force the Plains Indians to move away from the trails.

↓

> This meant the US Army was now helping white Americans to cross the Indian Frontier.

↓

> Then in 1851 the US government passed the **Indian Appropriations Act**. This started to move Indians onto reservations* within Indian Territory.

Figure: Events leading to the Indian Appropriations Act.

Exam-style question, Section A

Write a narrative account analysing the ways in which the US government policy towards the Plains Indians developed in the period 1835–51.

You may use the following in your answer:

- the Permanent Indian Frontier (c1834)
- the Indian Appropriations Act (1851).

You **must** also use information of your own. **8 marks**

Exam tip

Plan your answer first by listing the main developments of 1835–51 in sequence. This will help you link one event to another.

Summary

- The Plains Indians were made up of many different tribes and nations, with some very different customs.
- The Plains Indians' ideas about land, nature, warfare and property were very different from those of the white Americans who were starting to settle on the Plains.
- The US government supported the westward expansion of the USA. At first, tribes from the East were moved behind a Permanent Indian Frontier, then moved to live within reservations to keep them and white Americans apart.

Checkpoint

Strengthen

S1 Which of these came first: the Indian Appropriations Act, the end of the war with Mexico or the setting up of a Permanent Indian Frontier?

Challenge

C1 Explain the importance of the buffalo to the Plains Indians.

How confident do you feel about your answers to these questions? If you are not sure, it might help to start a timeline for the period covered by this chapter: from the 1830s to 1862.

1.2 Migration and early settlement

What factors encouraged migration west?

There were many different reasons why people decided to make the long and dangerous journey west. Some factors 'pushed' migrants away from the East, while others 'pulled' them to the West.

Key terms

Migration*
When large numbers of people (called **migrants**) go to live in another area or country.

Missionary*
Someone who travels to a place in order to get the people there to change their religion.

Pull factor

Farmland in Oregon
There was free, good quality farmland west of the Rocky Mountains.
People who were having a hard life in the East could start again in Oregon.

Push factor

Economic crisis in the East, 1837
Banks collapsed, people lost their jobs, wages fell, unemployment reached 25%. These all made people think about starting a new life in the West.

Pull factor

The Gold Rush in 1849
Gold was discovered in the mountains of California! Around 100,000 people left the East in 1849 to try to find gold in the West.

Factors that encouraged migration to the West

Pull factor

The Oregon Trail
This trail made it easier to get through the Rocky Mountains to Oregon and California. It was used from 1836. People could load a wagon with all their possessions and travel the Oregon Trail, instead of going by sea which took a long time and was expensive.

Push factor

Farming crisis in the East, 1837
Corn prices fell, and farmers lost their money. Farmland was also overcrowded. These all made people think about starting a new life in the West.

Figure: Factors that encouraged migration.

The Oregon Trail

- This route through the Rocky Mountains first became known in 1825.
- The first people to travel the Oregon Trail in a wagon were missionaries*. They made the trip in 1836.
- In 1840 the first family made the trip – the Walker family (including five children).

- In 1843, 900 people used the Oregon Trail: this was called the 'Great Emigration'.

The 'Great Emigration' was important because it showed that large numbers of people could make the journey and arrive safely. This encouraged more people to travel West.

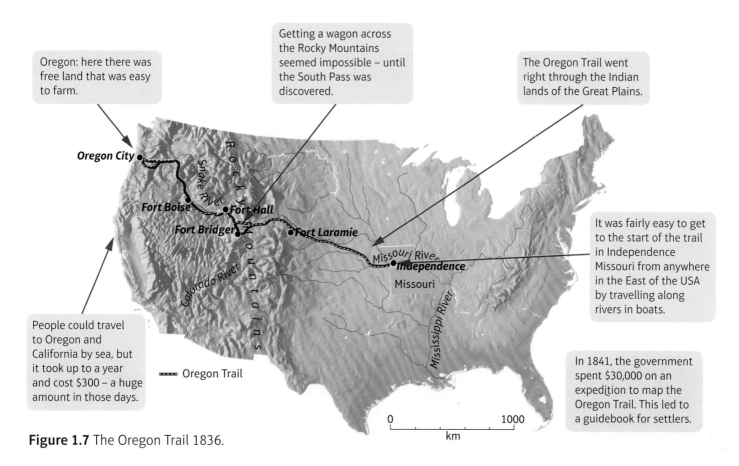

Oregon: here there was free land that was easy to farm.

Getting a wagon across the Rocky Mountains seemed impossible – until the South Pass was discovered.

The Oregon Trail went right through the Indian lands of the Great Plains.

It was fairly easy to get to the start of the trail in Independence Missouri from anywhere in the East of the USA by travelling along rivers in boats.

People could travel to Oregon and California by sea, but it took up to a year and cost $300 – a huge amount in those days.

In 1841, the government spent $30,000 on an expedition to map the Oregon Trail. This led to a guidebook for settlers.

═══ Oregon Trail

Figure 1.7 The Oregon Trail 1836.

Government help

Before 1846, the US government encouraged people to move to Oregon so that it could become US territory. By 1846, more than 5,000 people had migrated west along the Oregon Trail.

The Gold Rush of 1849

In 1848 gold was discovered in California's Sierra Nevada mountains. Hundreds of thousands of people travelled to the West in the hope of finding gold. By 1855, California's population had increased from almost nothing to 300,000 people because of the Gold Rush!

- Thousands travelled along the Oregon Trail to California.
- People who came looking for gold were called prospectors*.
- Not many people did find gold. But a lot of the prospectors settled down in California, for example as farmers.
- Businesses in California did very well by selling things that prospectors needed, such as equipment, food and drink, and entertainment.

Figure: Consequences of the Gold Rush.

Key term

Prospector*

Someone who searches for gold or other precious metals. They look for signs of the metals in rocky outcrops or in the silt of streams and river beds.

Manifest Destiny

Manifest Destiny* was the belief that white Americans had a special right to populate all areas of America.

- White Americans believed Manifest Destiny was what God wanted to happen for America.
- Ideas about Manifest Destiny encouraged people to travel to the West and settle there.

Source A

In 1860, the US government asked the artist Emanuel Leutze to paint a picture that put the concept of 'Manifest Destiny' into visual form. The picture's title is *Westward the course of Empire takes its way*.

Manifest Destiny encouraged white settlers to move West because it made people feel part of something important

Consequences of Manifest Destiny

Manifest Destiny could not happen unless American Indians gave up land

Figure: Manifest Destiny.

Key term

Manifest Destiny*

The belief that it was God's will for white people to take possession of the whole of the USA and make it productive and civilised.

Activities

1 The following events, dates and consequences have been muddled up. Sort them so that each event is with its correct date and a consequence that follows on from it.

Event	Date	Consequence
Gold is discovered in California.	1836	This starts the use of the Oregon Trail by migrants.
Financial crisis in the USA.	1837	A guidebook about using the Oregon Trail helps large groups of people to migrate west.
Government pays for an expedition to map the Oregon Trail.	1841	100,000 people travel to California in 1849 by land.
The first migrants reach Oregon.	1848	Unemployment and low wages mean many people are desperate for a new start in the West.

2 After reading through all the factors that encouraged people to migrate west, which one do you think was the most important, and why? Discuss this with a partner.

3 Study Source A with a partner. Describe what you can see happening in the painting. Whereabouts on the Oregon Trail do you think this scene is from?

The process and problems of migration

The Oregon Trail was 3,200 km long. Migrants using the Oregon Trail and then heading to California had a 3,800 km trip. The journey was very hard and migrants needed to plan each stage carefully.

How to survive the Oregon Trail

✓ Make sure you complete your journey before winter. Otherwise you'll get stuck in the snow in the mountains and may die of cold or starvation.

✓ Don't start the journey until April. Otherwise there won't be enough grass for your animals and they will starve.

✓ Make sure you take everything you need for your new life – without overloading your wagon. Take barrels of salt pork to live on – that won't go bad.

✓ Oxen are the best at pulling wagons all the way to Oregon. But they are slow! Don't delay on the way or you won't make it through the mountains before winter.

✓ Travel as a big group in a wagon train*. That way you can look after each other. Make sure you have someone who can fix the wagons, good hunters and someone with medical skills in your group.

Figure: How to stay safe on the Oregon Trail.

Problems

The main problems of migrating West along the Oregon Trail were:

- getting stuck where tracks became too difficult to pass along.
- falling ill – cholera* was the biggest killer; migrants used the same spots along rivers to camp so the river water became dirty if people used the river to go to the toilet.
- running out of supplies.
- being crushed by wagon wheels.
- drowning in river water.

Migrants feared attacks by Plains Indians, but, in fact, Plains Indians were more likely to help migrants than attack them. However, white settlers' fears led to calls for the government to protect migrants (see page 27 for more on this).

The experiences of the Donner Party

The Donner Party was a group of 300 migrants, in 60 wagons. The group, led by the Donner brothers, started the Oregon Trail in May 1846.

When they reached Fort Bridger in the Rocky Mountains in July, the group split. Around 80 migrants, including both Donner brothers, decided to try a new short cut that left the Oregon Trail. A trail guide had written about this short cut. He described it as a fine road with plenty of grass and water. What the migrants did not know was that the trail guide had not used this short cut himself.

Instead of saving time, the route caused many delays.

- Unlike the Oregon Trail, this route had not been marked out and was hard to follow.
- The land was rugged and rocky, with steep slopes and deep canyons. The party had to try out different spots to cross rivers before they found the safest place.
- There were also stretches of desert with no water or grass for the livestock*. There was nowhere to buy new provisions.

The group argued as to what they should do – keep going or turn back. It was mid-October when the Donner Party reached the Sierra Nevada Mountains.

Key terms

Wagon train*
A long line of wagons, carrying the settlers and their belongings.

Cholera*
A serious disease usually caused by drinking infected water.

Livestock*
Animals that are used in farming, such as cattle.

21

At the start of November, the exhausted oxen had dragged the wagons high into the mountains, but before they could make it over the pass, snowstorms trapped the Donner Party. Their livestock died and soon their food ran out. The first migrant died of starvation on 15 December. By the time rescuers reached the party in February, only half of the original 80 were alive – and most of those had only survived by eating those who had died.

Source B

Captain Fellun, who led one of the rescue parties, described what he found when he reached the Donner Party in February 1847.

```
A horrible scene presented itself. Human
bodies terribly mutilated, legs, arms and
skulls scattered in every direction. At the
mouth of a tent stood a large pot, filled with
human flesh cut up. It was the body of George
Donner. His head had been split open and the
brains extracted.
```

The Mormon migration, 1846–47

The experiences of the **Mormons*** were different from the Donner Party, even though they also split away from the main Oregon Trail.

Other Christians did not like the Mormons because of their beliefs (for example, Mormons believed men could have several wives).

In 1845, the Mormons were ordered to leave Illinois after their leader, Joseph Smith, was murdered. Their new leader, Brigham Young, believed God had called on the Mormons to migrate to Salt Lake Valley, south of the Oregon Trail, and build a town there. Salt Lake Valley was outside US territory at that time and the Mormons hoped they could escape persecution there.

Planning the Mormon migration

Brigham Young's leadership was very important in the success of the migration. He led the first group to prepare the trail to Salt Lake Valley. He also planned carefully for how the second, much larger wagon train, should make the trip.

Key term

Mormons*
Members of a religious organisation called the Church of the Latter Day Saints that began in 1830 in the USA.

The Mormons left Illinois in February 1846. They slowly travelled to Omaha, where a branch of the Oregon Trail began. It took until June for all the Mormons to get there.

↓

Brigham Young decided June was too late to begin their journey. They stayed at Omaha until the next spring. They suffered through a very cold winter.

↓

In April 1847, a small group of 150 Mormons set off for Salt Lake Valley. Brigham Young led this group. They took plenty of food and supplies, and a boat, to help them cross rivers.

↓

The small group followed the same route as the Donner Party. As they went, they marked the trail and the best places to cross rivers and find water. They even planted vegetables at places along the route for future settlers!

↓

Young's small group reached Salt Lake Valley in July 1847. A much bigger group of 1,500 Mormons had set off from Omaha by then. Thanks to the first group, they had a clear route to follow.

↓

The second big group of Mormons reached Salt Lake Valley in August 1847.

↓

Between 1847 and 1869, 70,000 Mormons followed the **Mormon Trail** to Salt Lake Valley.

Figure: The Mormon Trail.

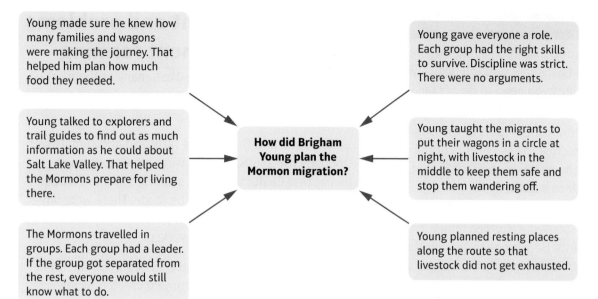

Young made sure he knew how many families and wagons were making the journey. That helped him plan how much food they needed.

Young talked to explorers and trail guides to find out as much information as he could about Salt Lake Valley. That helped the Mormons prepare for living there.

The Mormons travelled in groups. Each group had a leader. If the group got separated from the rest, everyone would still know what to do.

How did Brigham Young plan the Mormon migration?

Young gave everyone a role. Each group had the right skills to survive. Discipline was strict. There were no arguments.

Young taught the migrants to put their wagons in a circle at night, with livestock in the middle to keep them safe and stop them wandering off.

Young planned resting places along the route so that livestock did not get exhausted.

Figure: How Young planned the Mormon migration.

Meeting the challenges of Salt Lake Valley

The Great Salt Lake, and the land surrounding it, was a harsh, dry landscape. The lake itself was salty, and the land was too poor to grow crops on.

Under Young's leadership, the Mormons built a successful settlement. This happened because the Mormons worked together to one central plan, under strict leadership.

1 The Mormons believed that Young was God's prophet* and they obeyed him completely. Young decided that the Church owned all the land: no individual owned anything. Also, everyone must work together to help each other.

2 The Mormons built irrigation* systems from the freshwater streams that ran into the Great Salt Lake. This meant they had water to grow crops.

3 In order that the Mormons would have all the different products they needed, new settlements were planned and each one was designed to produce particular products, such as food crops, minerals or timber. Each settlement had a church leader with authority over everything.

4 New Mormon settlements spread out away from Salt Lake Valley, into areas with better water supplies. Products from these settlements (such as vegetables, flour, timber and metals) were brought back to Great Salt Lake City, founded by Young.

Source C

A painting by William Henry Jackson showing Mormon settlers heading to Utah and Salt Lake Valley in the 1850s.

Source D

A description of Salt Lake Valley, written by one of the first settlers.

A broad and barren [lifeless] plain hemmed in by mountains, blistering in the burning rays of the midsummer sun. No waving fields, no swaying forests, no green meadows. But on all sides a seemingly endless waste of sagebrush — the paradise of the lizard, the cricket [grasshopper] and the rattlesnake.

Key terms

Prophet*
A person believed to be sent by God.

Irrigation*
Supplying water to land to grow crops.

Activities ?

1. In pairs, plan a group migration along the Oregon Trail. Identify the challenges you will be likely to meet, and the things you need to do or take with you to meet these challenges.

2. Write your own newspaper report of the Donner Party disaster. Describe the key events of their journey. Explain the mistakes they made that turned their trip into a disaster.

3. Write a paragraph comparing the Donner Party disaster with the successful Mormon migration. Aim to make three points. Here is one to get you started: 'While the Donner Party argued about which way to go, the Mormons followed Brigham Young's leadership without question.'

Exam-style question, Section A

Explain **two** consequences of the setting up of the Oregon Trail (1836). **8 marks**

Exam tip

A consequence is something that happens as a result of an event. Your answer should focus on consequences; there are no marks here for describing the Oregon Trail.

The development and problems of white settlement farming

When migrants reached the West, many of them set up farms. They had come west to settle on land of their own – they were settlers.

In California and Oregon, the farmland and climate were good. By the 1850s, farmers were growing so much wheat that California began sending grain to Europe. There was a lot of money to be made. There were large farms that could afford steam-powered farm machinery and which employed many workers.

By the 1850s, settlement had also begun on the Great Plains. In 1854, the US government created two new territories, Kansas and Nebraska. These territories were behind the Permanent Indian Frontier. Now the US government opened them for settlement by white Americans.

However, no one knew which crops to grow on the Great Plains or how best to prepare the land.

Source E

This picture from the 1850s shows a Californian farmer ploughing his fields in mild November weather.

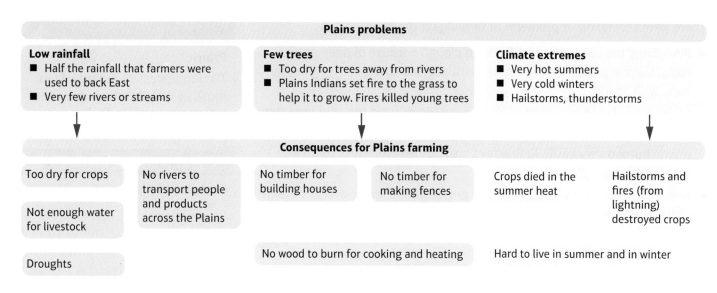

Plains problems

Low rainfall	**Few trees**	**Climate extremes**
■ Half the rainfall that farmers were used to back East ■ Very few rivers or streams	■ Too dry for trees away from rivers ■ Plains Indians set fire to the grass to help it to grow. Fires killed young trees	■ Very hot summers ■ Very cold winters ■ Hailstorms, thunderstorms

Consequences for Plains farming

Too dry for crops	No rivers to transport people and products across the Plains	No timber for building houses	No timber for making fences	Crops died in the summer heat	Hailstorms and fires (from lightning) destroyed crops
Not enough water for livestock					
Droughts		No wood to burn for cooking and heating		Hard to live in summer and in winter	

Figure 1.8 Farming on the Great Plains was very difficult for the settlers.

With no wood for fuel, settlers burned buffalo 'chips': buffalo dung that had dried in the Sun. Buffalo dung burned very quickly so a lot was needed to keep the house heated in winter.

On the Great Plains, water could be 300 feet down. Wells were expensive to dig and getting enough water for people, animals and crops each day was hard work.

With no trees for timber, settlers made houses out of 'sods' of earth Sod houses were warm and fire-proof, but were always dirty, infested with insects and started to turn back into mud in heavy rain.

Families were often miles away from any other settlers, making life on the Great Plains very lonely. The nearest town could be several days of travel away.

Figure 1.9 Settlers, like this Kansas family, faced tough living and working conditions.

Activity ?

List four problems the white settlers faced as they tried to farm on the Great Plains. Decide which was the most important and why.

There were several other problems of farming on the Plains.

- Ploughing: the soil was very difficult to plough because of deep grass roots. Normal ploughs broke. Farmers usually had to dig up the grass by hand with spades.
- Crops: crops failed because the Plains were too dry and too cold in winter.
- Prairie* fires: after a long, hot and dry summer, the long grass of the prairie burned very easily. Prairie fires also burned crops and could kill livestock and people.
- Grasshoppers: some years, millions of grasshoppers swept over the Plains destroying crops, grass, and even the wool on sheep's backs. Grasshopper droppings turned everything brown and polluted any water sources.

Key term

Prairie*
The large areas of flat grassland, mostly without trees, of the Great Plains region of North America.

Extend your knowledge

Grasshopper 'plagues'

Most parts of the Great Plains had at least one grasshopper 'plague' every ten years. The worst outbreak was in 1874, when 120 billion insects damaged over 300,000 km² of land.

Summary

- Different factors encouraged migration to the West. Some factors 'pushed' migrants to leave the East and some 'pullled' them to the West.
- The Oregon Trail made migration to the West possible, but it was a hard journey. Sometimes it was disastrous, as with the Donner Party.
- Early settlers had a hard life on the Great Plains. They were unable to farm successfully there.

Checkpoint

Strengthen

S1 400,000 people had followed the Oregon Trail by 1869. Which **one** of the following factors do you think was the most important in encouraging migration west along the Trail? a) the economic crisis of 1837, b) the discovery of gold in California, c) beliefs about 'Manifest Destiny'? Briefly explain your answer.

S2 Many people died following the Oregon Trail – around 20,000 between 1840 and 1860. What was the most common cause of death and how was it linked to the difficulties of following the Trail?

Challenge

C1 Explain two of the problems facing white settlers trying to farm on the Great Plains.

How confident do you feel about your answers to these questions? To build your confidence, add key events to your timeline (see page 17). Practise making links between the events – for example, how could you link the Indian Appropriations Act of 1851 with the US government opening up Kansas and Nebraska for settlement in 1854?

1.3 Conflict and tension

Learning outcomes

- Understand the reason for tension between settlers and Plains Indians, and the significance of the Fort Laramie Treaty (1851).
- Understand the problem of lawlessness in the West and what was done to tackle it.

Tension between settlers and Plains Indians

Life for both settlers and Plains Indians was very hard in the West. One bad decision or accident could put a group of settlers or a band of Plains Indians at great risk. This made settlers and Plains Indians very worried about possible threats.

White fear of Plains Indians

Plains Indians often raided other tribes to steal food, horses and people. When white settlers, travelling the Oregon Trail, saw Plains Indians on their way to raids, they often thought the war parties were threatening to attack them. Actually, Plains Indian attacks on migrants were rare, but white settlers scared each other with stories of attacks. White settlers were very afraid that Plains Indians would attack them, scalp* the men and carry the women and children off into slavery.

White settlers had strongly racist views about American Indians. Most were certain that the white race was naturally superior to the American Indian race.

Key terms

Scalp*

The cutting off of the hair and skin from the top of an enemy's head to keep as a trophy and as a sign of bravery. Both the Plains Indians and white Americans did this.

Stampede*

When a group of large animals suddenly starts running in the same direction because they are frightened.

Some settlers used Plains Indian experience and knowledge about their environment. The Mormon settlers, for example, learned a lot about how to survive from studying crops and farming methods used by the Plains Indians. Some Plains Indians went to live among white people. However, most white Americans and Plains Indians had very little understanding of each other. This led to mistrust.

Interpretation 1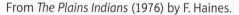

From *The Plains Indians* (1976) by F. Haines.

When the trail to Oregon was opened to wagon trains in the early 1840s, the resulting annual flow of travellers brought critical new problems to the Indian tribes… friction between the travellers and the tribes soon built up to danger point, and minor conflicts erupted all along the way. Most problems… resulted directly from the white man's firm belief that an Indian had no rights of any kind, even in his own land.

Threats to Plains Indian food supply

The discovery of gold in California meant thousands of white migrants travelled along the Oregon Trail in 1849 and 1850. This led to serious problems for Plains Indians along the Trail.

- The migrants killed large numbers of buffalo for meat. The Plains Indian way of hunting buffalo depended on managing the herd carefully, but the migrants scared the buffalo and caused stampedes*.

- The thousands of oxen and livestock belonging to the migrants meant a shortage of grass for the animals the Plains Indians hunted.
- Generally the Plains Indians did not attack the migrants but they did keep an eye on them. The migrants thought the Plains Indians were going to attack them, so they demanded that forts were built along the Trail to protect migrants.

Figure 1.10 Key events leading to the Fort Laramie Treaty (1851).

The Fort Laramie Treaty (1851)

The US government was worried about the growing tension between migrants and Plains Indians. It organised a council of Plains Indian tribes from the northern Great Plains. The government wanted the tribes to agree to a **treaty*** that would end conflicts between the tribes and guarantee the safety of migrants. The negotiators also wanted to get the tribes to agree to live in fixed territories.

The council was held near Fort Laramie. The treaty the government wanted the Plains Indians to sign was called the Fort Laramie Treaty. But there were problems in getting agreement, which had consequences for the Treaty's success.

> **Key term**
>
> **Treaty***
> A written agreement made between two or more peoples, or governments.

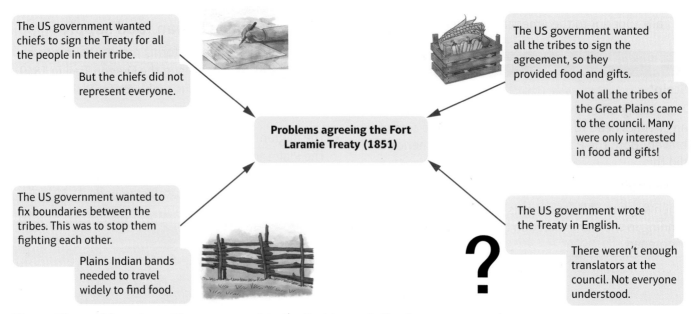

Figure: The problems in getting agreement to the Fort Laramie Treaty.

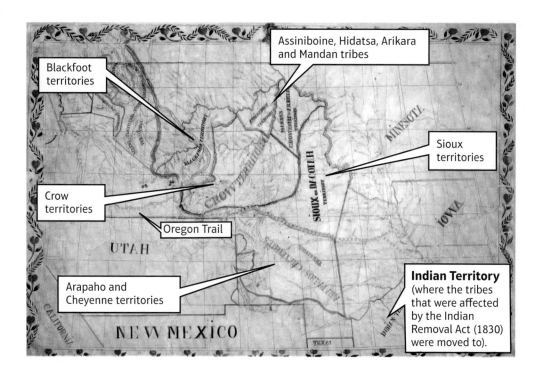

Figure 1.11 The map produced by the Fort Laramie Treaty in 1851. It shows the boundaries of each tribe's territory. The route of the Oregon Trail has been added and labels make the map clearer.

Treaty agreements

On 17 September 1851, the Treaty was finally signed by the council members, after more than a week of negotiations. The main terms of the Treaty were:

The Plains Indians would:	The US government would:
end the fighting between the tribes	protect Plains Indians from white Americans (including migrants trying to settle on Plains Indian land)
allow migrants to travel through their lands in safety	
allow surveyors* from railroad companies to enter their lands in safety	
allow the government to build roads through their lands and build army posts	pay the tribes an annuity* (a yearly payment) of $50,000 as long as the Treaty terms were kept to
pay compensation* if any individuals from their tribe broke the Treaty terms (e.g. by attacking migrants)	

Key terms

Surveyor*

Someone whose job it is to measure and mark out areas of land.

Compensation*

Money paid to someone because they have been injured or something of theirs has been damaged.

Annuity*

A fixed amount of money that is paid to someone each year.

Key term

Reservation*

An area of land 'reserved' for use by American Indians and managed by the government.

Exam-style question, Section A

Explain **two** consequences of the Fort Laramie Treaty (1851).

8 marks

Exam tip

The question wants you to explain the results of something, in other words: what difference did it make? Use phrases such as 'as a result' or 'the effect of this was' in your answer to show the consequences of the event in the question.

Significance of the Treaty

- Mapping areas 'belonging' to each tribe was a first step towards moving Indians onto reservations*. (The Fort Laramie Treaty did not set up reservations itself, however.)
- The Treaty stated that migrants must be allowed to travel safely across the Plains. This meant that the Permanent Indian Frontier in the northern Plains no longer stopped white Americans from crossing into American Indian areas (see page 17).
- The US government introduced annuities, paid in food and products, to compensate Plains Indians for allowing migrants across their lands. In the future, the government refused to pay this unless tribes did what it wanted.

Problems with the Treaty

- Although individual chiefs had signed the Treaty, each band within a tribe made its own decision whether to follow it or not.
- Not all the Plains Indian representatives understood what they had signed up to, due to translation difficulties and because of different ideas about land as property.
- When the Sioux complained that their hunting grounds were larger than those shown on the map, the government said that all Plains Indians were still free to hunt in other tribes' territories. So the boundaries were not seen as being very important.

The result of these problems was that neither side stuck to the Treaty terms for very long.

- Plains Indian bands continued to fight each other, which the US government saw as breaking the Treaty.
- Migrants did not stick to the Oregon Trail but went into areas that Plains Indians viewed as off limits. The US Army did nothing to stop this.

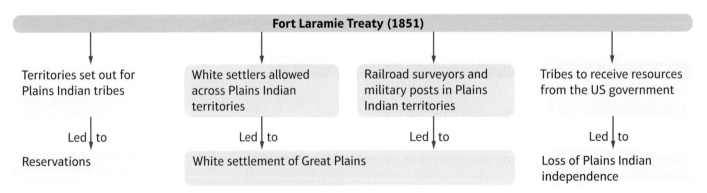

Figure 1.12 Key consequences of the Fort Laramie Treaty (1851).

The problems of lawlessness in early towns and settlements

Law and order

The American West is often described as being '**lawless**'. This does not mean that there were not any laws. Instead, the problem was making people obey the laws. This is called law enforcement.

Most people wanted law enforcement in the West to protect them from thieves and cheats and from violence.

The problem was, the official law enforcement system was not big enough to cover the West.

The impact of mass settlement

During the early 1840s, the numbers of migrants to the West were very small. Lawless behaviour was minimal.

The situation changed with the California Gold Rush. The white American population of California in 1846 was around 8,000. By 1855, there were 300,000 people, including people from all over the world. This mass migration* and mass settlement* created problems that overwhelmed the systems of law enforcement in California.

Key terms
Mass migration*
When very large numbers of people migrate.
Mass settlement*
When very large numbers of people come to live in an area.
Claim*
A legal document stating that someone is taking control over an area of land.
Corruption*
Dishonest and illegal behaviour, especially by someone with power over other people.

The gold prospectors gathered wherever gold was found. Camps grew up in days from nothing to huge tent cities of thousands of men. Serious problems quickly arose.

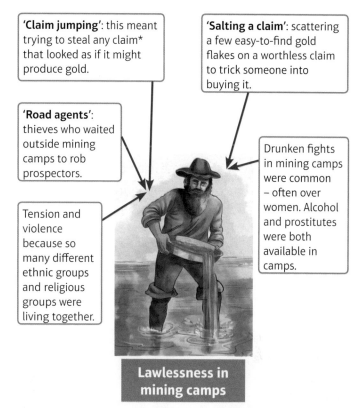

'**Claim jumping**': this meant trying to steal any claim* that looked as if it might produce gold.

'**Salting a claim**': scattering a few easy-to-find gold flakes on a worthless claim to trick someone into buying it.

'**Road agents**': thieves who waited outside mining camps to rob prospectors.

Drunken fights in mining camps were common – often over women. Alcohol and prostitutes were both available in camps.

Tension and violence because so many different ethnic groups and religious groups were living together.

Lawlessness in mining camps

Figure: Problems with lawlessness in the mining camps.

Gangs and racism

In 1849, the population of San Francisco rapidly increased from 1,000 to 25,000. The growth continued in the 1850s:

- By mid-1850, many prospectors had found nothing or had 'worked out' their claim and could not find any more gold. Many of these disappointed men went to San Francisco to look for jobs.

- Many of the thousands of disappointed prospectors who returned to San Francisco could not find work.

- This caused a crime wave in the town in 1851. Rival gangs took control of city areas.

- The law officers in the town were unable to do anything because of both the size of the problem and corruption*.

- Lawlessness reached the point where gang members would stroll into saloons, kill people, take their money, and leave.

Another cause of lawlessness was racism.

- In 1852, a famine in China led to a huge increase in Chinese migrants coming to California: from 2,000 in 1851 to 20,000 in 1852. Racism against Chinese immigrants increased.
- Chinese miners were prevented from working new claims: they were only permitted to work old claims.
- However, by hard work, Chinese miners still made money.
- Jealous of their success, white Americans robbed them, destroyed their camps and sometimes even murdered Chinese people.

Source A

This picture from 1855 shows a California saloon filled with Chinese, European and Mexican customers.

Attempts by government and local communities to tackle lawlessness
Federal law enforcement and the sheriff
The territories of the West were under the control of the federal government.

The federal government decided on the laws for each territory. It also appointed a governor for the territory, three judges to hear court cases, and a US marshal* who was responsible for law enforcement. The marshal could appoint deputies to help him and could also order any man to join a posse* to hunt down lawbreakers.

Once a territory had a population of 5,000 people, communities could elect a sheriff* for their county. The sheriff had similar powers to the US marshal for this county area. Sheriffs had no legal training but kept order as best they could.

Key terms

US marshal*

A police officer in charge of a district. A US marshal was a federal law officer appointed to an area.

Posse*

A group of men called together by a sheriff or marshal to help him in enforcing the law.

Sheriff*

An elected law officer with the responsibility of keeping the peace in his area and carrying out orders of a law court, such as making arrests and delivering prisoners to jail.

There were some major problems with this system of law and order.

Corruption – sheriffs were not paid much. Sometimes, criminals could pay a bribe for the sheriff to leave them alone.

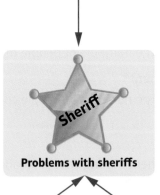

Problems with sheriffs

Geography – sheriffs often had to cover huge areas. News of lawbreaking could take a long time to reach the sheriff.

No legal training – this meant sheriffs were often unfair, for example by looking after their friends first. This caused tensions.

Figure: Problems with law enforcement.

Settling claim disputes in mining camps

- Mining communities got together to agree and write down the rules that would govern mining in their district.
- A recorder was chosen to record all the claims that were made and who had claimed them.
- A respected community member was chosen to be the judge in a miners' court. He judged disputes and said what should happen. Juries were often appointed as well.

Vigilance committees

The crime wave in San Francisco in 1851 produced a new form of law enforcement: the vigilance committee – better known as vigilantes*.

- Townspeople got together to organise their own law enforcement because they felt the government law enforcement wasn't working.
- They created a vigilance committee of about 200 people.
- These vigilantes rounded up suspected criminals, decided whether they were guilty, and carried out punishments.

Key term

Vigilantes*

A group of ordinary citizens who punish suspected lawbreakers themselves instead of relying on the official justice system (usually because it is inadequate).

The idea of vigilance committees spread rapidly through the mining camps in the West.

A problem with the vigilance committees was that people were not usually given a fair trial: a person's guilt was usually decided before they were captured. This often led to the lynching* of suspects. Another problem was that the violence quickly got out of control. Vigilance committees used their power to get rid of people they didn't like. The situation often ended up even worse than before.

Key term

Lynching*

This occurs when a group of people takes the law into their own hands and executes someone they suspect of a crime (usually by hanging).

Source B

This picture, from 1892, shows a lynch mob coming to hang a murderer in a mining settlement. It is a reproduction of a painting made in 1848.

Dealing with racist crimes

Racist attacks increased as a result of mass settlement in California. Unfortunately, the state government was also racist. For example, California's state government passed a law that taxed Chinese miners more than the US citizens. Another law said that Chinese people could not be witnesses in court. This meant that crimes against Chinese people went unpunished.

Activity ?

Using Figure 1.13 to help you, identify three factors that encouraged communities in the West to set up vigilance committees rather than rely on state or federal law enforcement.

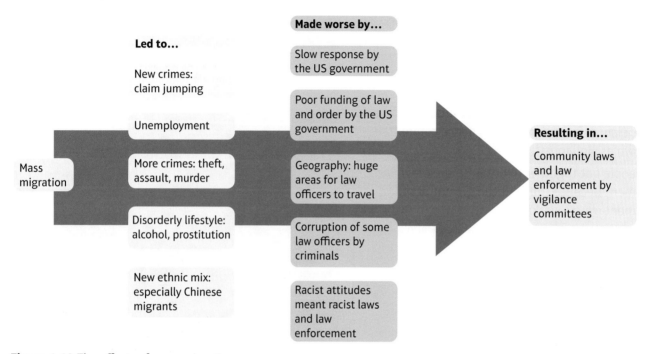

Figure 1.13 The effects of mass migration.

Summary

- The growing number of settlers moving on to the Plains led to conflict between settlers and Plains Indians.
- The Fort Laramie Treaty (1851) involved promises being made by both the Plains Indians and the government.
- Law and order was difficult to enforce in the early towns and settlements. In some settlements, a lack of government help meant local communities tried tackling lawlessness themselves.

Checkpoint

Strengthen

S1 What size population did a territory need to reach before sheriffs could be elected there?

S2 Describe how a vigilance committee (vigilante group) tackled lawlessness.

Challenge

C1 Describe three problems with the way the Fort Laramie Treaty (1851) was agreed. (Hint: different ideas about chiefs, different ideas about land.)

How confident do you feel about your answers to these questions? One way you could boost your understanding is to write down the key terms from the topic and see how many connections you can make between them. For example, what connects: 'sheriff' and 'posse'?

Recap: The early settlement of the West, c1835–c1862

Recall quiz

1 Give three uses of the buffalo by the Plains Indians.
2 In 1848, the USA gained new territories in the West due to its victory over which country?
3 Identify two problems for settlers on the Plains due to the lack of trees.
4 In what year was the Indian Appropriations Act passed by the US government?
5 What happened in 1837 that acted to 'push' some white settlers from the East to the West?
6 Identify a (bad) decision that led to the Donner Party disaster.
7 Identify three reasons why the Mormons were able to survive in the Great Salt Lake region.
8 'The Fort Laramie Treaty of 1851 created reservations for the Plains Indians of the northern Plains.' Is that statement true or false?
9 Write a definition of 'Manifest Destiny'.
10 What did the US government hope to achieve by creating a Permanent Indian Frontier?

Activities

1 Figure 1.14 shows a map of the USA in 1861. There are two arrows on it, representing pressures on the Plains Indians from the East and also from the West. Sketch a copy of the map and add text to the two arrows explaining the factors putting pressure on the Plains Indians in the period 1835 to 1862.

2 Many different factors encouraged settlement in the West. List three and decide which one of these was most important. Make sure you can explain why.

Exam-style question, Section A

Explain **two** of the following:

- The importance of the Oregon Trail for the early settlement of the West.
- The importance of the Indian Appropriations Act (1851) for the way of life of the Plains Indians.
- The importance of the development of new mining towns for law and order in the early West. **16 marks**

Exam tip

Although three bullet points are listed, the question only asks you to pick two of them for your answer. You should pick the two you can answer best and write two separate answers for this question. Pay careful attention to what exactly you are being asked to explain: the second part of each bullet point gives you the specific focus of the question.

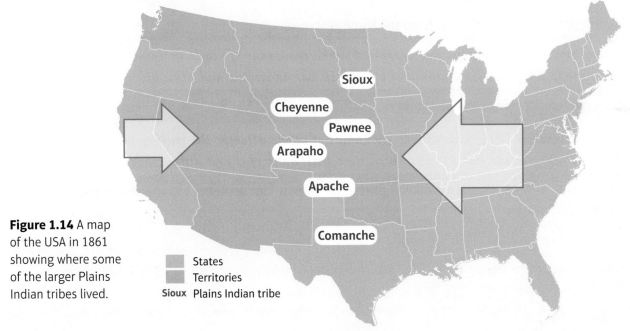

Figure 1.14 A map of the USA in 1861 showing where some of the larger Plains Indian tribes lived.

- States
- Territories
- **Sioux** Plains Indian tribe

Writing historically: building information

When you are asked to write an explanation or analysis, you need to provide as much detailed information as possible.

Learning outcomes

By the end of this lesson, you will understand how to:

- use relative clauses to add clear and detailed information to your writing
- use noun phrases in apposition to add clear and detailed information to your writing.

Definitions

Relative clause: a clause that adds information or modifies a noun.

Noun phrase in apposition: two noun phrases, positioned side-by-side, the second adding information to the first, e.g. '[1] San Francisco, [2] the port city where many migrants arrived in California, grew rapidly between 1849 and 1855.'

How can I add detail to my writing?

Look at a sentence from the response below to this exam-style question:

> Explain the importance of the discovery of gold in California (1848) for the settlement of the American West. **(8 marks)**

> *Many of the miners, who had failed to find gold, settled in California as farmers.*

The main clause is highlighted in yellow. The relative clause is highlighted in purple.

This noun phrase is changed by this **relative clause**: it provides more information about the miners.

1. How could you rewrite the sentence above as two separate sentences?

2. Why do you think the writer chose to use a main clause and a relative clause instead of writing them as two separate sentences?

Now look at these four sentences taken from the same response:

> *Gold was discovered in 1848. This was enough to make thousands of people attempt the journey west. They made the journey overland and by sea. It was dangerous and difficult.*

Look at this new version using relative clauses.

> *Gold was discovered in 1848, which made thousands of people attempt the journey west. They made the journey overland and by sea, which were both dangerous and difficult.*

3. Which version of the information do you prefer: the one in four sentences or the one in two sentences? Explain your answer.

How can I add detail to my writing in different ways?

You can also add detail to a sentence using a **noun phrase in apposition**.

Compare these sentences:

> *Migration to the West,* which was a long and dangerous journey, *was attempted by thousands of people in search of a fortune in gold.*

This uses a relative clause to add information clearly and briefly.

> *Migration to the West,* a long and dangerous journey, *was attempted by thousands of people in search of a fortune in gold.*

This uses a noun phrase in apposition to add the same information even more clearly and briefly.

4. How could you combine the information in the pair of sentences below using a noun phrase in apposition?

> *San Francisco became the largest city on the West Coast in 1849. It had been a small settlement before the gold rush.*

5. Now try rewriting these two sentences into one sentence using a noun phrase in apposition (hint: start your noun phrase in apposition after 'settling in the West').

> *The mass migration of 1849 showed that settling in the West was achievable. It had seemed very difficult before then.*

Did you notice?

If you remove the relative clause or the noun phrase in apposition from the sentences above, they both still make sense. They are also both separated from the rest of the sentence with commas.

Improving an answer

Look at the extract below from another response to the exam question on the previous page:

> *The Gold Rush led to a sudden rush of migrants to California. It was a major factor in making the West seem like a good place to live. The rapid increase in population of miners led to the creation and growth of towns. The miners needed food, shops, transport and equipment. This added to the growth of towns as shopkeepers and traders also settled in them. The shopkeepers and traders sold the miners what they needed.*

6. a. Rewrite the information in the answer above, making it as clear and brief as possible. You could use:

- relative clauses
- nouns in apposition.

b. Look carefully at your response to Question 6a. Are all your sentences easy to read and understand, or are some of them too long and confusing? If so, try re-writing them to make their meaning as clear as possible.

02 | Development of the Plains, c1862–c1876

The American Civil War (1861–65) was between the northern states and the southern states of the USA. When the Civil War ended, more white settlers arrived on the Plains.

Railroads brought the new settlers and also supplied them with products made in the USA's big cities. Meanwhile, in the southern state of Texas, cattlemen wanted to find ways to sell their cattle to buyers in US cities. The new railroads were the key to this, and the cattle industry boomed into a 'beef bonanza'.

Ranching also began on the Plains, with enormous numbers of cattle roaming the 'open range', guarded and rounded up by cowboys living and working on the ranches.

As development on the Plains increased, conflicts between Plains Indians and the new settlers increased, too. The government continued to encourage Plains Indians to move to reservations where they would be 'protected', but problems led to 'Indian wars' between Plains Indian tribes and the US Army.

Learning outcomes

By the end of this chapter, you will:

- understand how the end of the American Civil War, government policies and the building of railroads all boosted the settlement of the Plains
- understand what caused the cattle industry to boom in the West, and how changes in the cattle industry affected the life of cowboys
- understand the impacts of the development of the Plains on the Plains Indians, and the conflicts that resulted with the US Army.

2.1 The development of settlement in the West

- Understand the consequences of the American Civil War for the West, including the effects of the Homestead Act and the Pacific Railroad Act.
- Understand the problems of law and order.

The significance of the American Civil War on the development of the West

> **The American Civil War: fact file**
>
> **Date:** 1861–65
> **Who was the war between?** The Confederacy (11 southern states which had left the USA) versus the Union (the remaining northern states of the USA)
> **Who won?** The Union
> **How many died?** 600,000
> **How many were wounded?** 400,000
> **Other impacts:**
> - Many of the Confederate (southern) states were badly damaged by the war.
> - All the former Confederate states came back to rejoin the USA after the war.
> - Slaves in the southern states were freed.

Figure 2.1 A fact files on the American Civil War.

After the Civil War the US government set about rebuilding the USA. This involved repairing the enormous destruction throughout the South, and giving US citizenship to former African American slaves.

The economic problems and social changes in the South, after the war, led many people to look at starting a new life in the West. Many of these people were ex-soldiers and former slaves. Settling in the West after the Civil War was easier due to laws passed by the US government during the war.

Government support for settlement in the West during the Civil War

Before the Civil War began, the US government was made up of representatives of southern states and representatives of northern states. North and South both had different ideas about the West.

> **Northern states** wanted new states in the West to be free of slavery. Northerners wanted family farms worked by free, independent people.

> **Southern states** relied on slave labour for their plantation farms. They wanted slavery to be legal in new states in the West, as it was legal in the South.

Figure: What the North and the South wanted to happen in the American West before the Civil War.

When the southern states left the USA in 1861 to set up the Confederacy (see fact file), it meant the US government was now controlled by the northern states. In 1862, the US government passed two important laws about what should happen in the West:

- **The Homestead Act** (May 1862) – aimed at settling the West with individual farms, owned and worked by free men and women.
- **The Pacific Railroad Act** (July 1862) – aimed at developing rail links between the new lands of the West and the northern industrial cities.

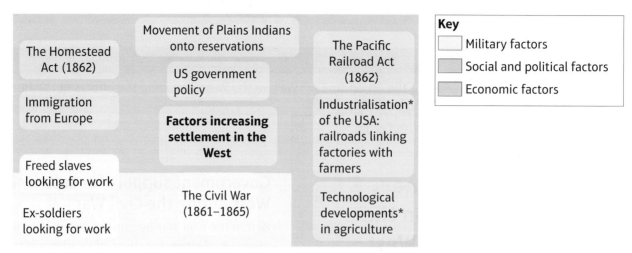

Figure 2.1 Key factors in settlement in the West, 1862–76.

The Homestead Act (1862)

The Homestead Act encouraged the settlement of the West. It encouraged people to take up land that had not been claimed in the West and build a new life there.

The Homestead Act gave away small plots of land in the West to ordinary people.

- The plots were 160-acre 'homesteads'. A homestead was a family house and enough land to support the family. People taking up homesteads were called homesteaders.
- It cost just $10 to make a claim to a homestead plot – this was called 'filing a claim'.

The US government did not want all the land in the West to be bought up by a few rich landowners. It wanted to encourage the settlement of the West by lots of individual farmers. Thousands of small farmers all paying property taxes to the government would give a big boost to the US economy.

Figure: How the Homestead Act worked.

The significance of the Homestead Act

Achievements

- By 1876, over six million acres of government land had become homesteads.

- Parts of the Great Plains were settled for the first time. Eventually, 80 million acres of public land were settled as a direct consequence of the Homestead Act. For example, in Nebraska nearly half the settled land was settled by homesteaders.

- The Homestead Act encouraged immigration from Europe. By 1875, more than half of Nebraska's population were recent immigrants and their children.

Limitations

- By 1884, only 13 million acres had become the legal property of homesteaders. By 1900, this figure had grown to 24 million acres. Sixty percent of claims failed because farming the land for five years was not easy.

- The government gave far more land to the railroads – 300 million acres compared to 80 million acres eventually given to homesteaders.

- More homesteads were formed by people buying land from the railroad companies than through the Homestead Act.

- Rich landowners did find ways to use the Homestead Act to get more land very cheaply. For example, big ranch owners would make all their employees file claims and then get them to hand over the rights to the land to the ranch owner.

- Many people filed claims in order to sell the land at a profit. It was possible to buy the land cheaply after just six months rather than waiting five years to get it for free. The land could then be sold on for a higher price. This meant the family that ended up farming the land had paid someone for it rather than getting it for free through the Homestead Act.

Activity ?

Study Source A, an advert to encourage people to settle as homesteaders in Nebraska.

   a Did the Homestead Act provide 'lands for the landless' and 'homes for the homeless'?

   b Why did the government 'almost donate' (i.e. give away free) millions of acres in the Homestead Act?

   c Explain one connection between the Homestead Act and the Civil War.

   d Why do you think the advert mentions that the land on offer is 'near some railroad'?

Source A

Part of a pamphlet from 1869 advertising the opportunities for homesteaders in Nebraska.

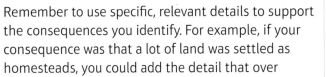

LANDS for the LANDLESS!
Homes for the Homeless!!
Millions of Acres almost donated to the brave Pioneers of the World by the generous government of America.
SOLDIERS
Of the war of 1861, come forward and take your Homesteads near some Railroad in
NEBRASKA.
For particulars address J. H. NOTEWARE, State Sup't of Immigration, Omaha. Neb.

Exam-style question, Section A

Explain **two** consequences of the Homestead Act (1862).   **8 marks**

Exam tip

Remember to use specific, relevant details to support the consequences you identify. For example, if your consequence was that a lot of land was settled as homesteads, you could add the detail that over six million acres were settled by homesteaders by 1876.

The Pacific Railroad Act (1862)

The Pacific Railroad Act encouraged the building of a railroad right across the continent of America – a transcontinental railway. The railroads:

- made migration to the West much easier
- encouraged the development of towns in the West
- boosted the sale of land to settlers
- linked up industrial cities in the north-east with farming areas in the West.

The First Transcontinental Railroad

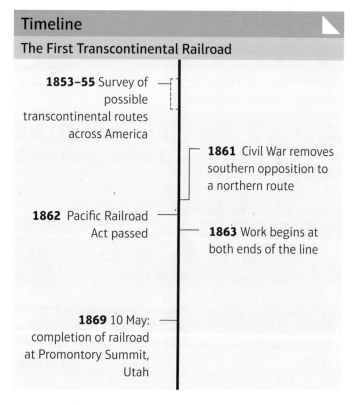

Timeline

The First Transcontinental Railroad

1853–55 Survey of possible transcontinental routes across America

1861 Civil War removes southern opposition to a northern route

1862 Pacific Railroad Act passed

1863 Work begins at both ends of the line

1869 10 May: completion of railroad at Promontory Summit, Utah

There were two main problems with building a railroad to link the eastern and western halves of the USA before 1862.

- Building a 2,000 km railroad was too difficult and expensive. No private company would risk it.
- The North and the South of the USA couldn't agree on the route of the railroad. The northern states wanted it to link California with Chicago. The southern states thought this would mean the South would miss out.

When the southern states left the Union in 1861, the US government was controlled by the northern states. The northern-controlled government chose a route that went from Sacramento, California, to Omaha, Nebraska. From Omaha, the First Transcontinental Railroad would link up with the existing eastern railroad network.

The Pacific Railroad Act split the job of building the First Transcontinental Railroad between two companies: the **Union Pacific** and the **Central Pacific**. The Pacific Railroad Act said the US government had to help the two companies by:

- getting rid of any rights Plains Indians might have to land along the route
- loaning each company $16,000 for every mile of track they laid ($48,000 for every mile that went through mountain areas because this was more expensive)
- giving each company large sections of public land along the railroad for them to sell.

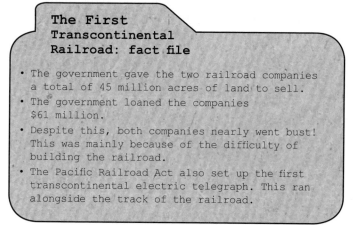

```
The First
Transcontinental
Railroad: fact file

• The government gave the two railroad companies
  a total of 45 million acres of land to sell.
• The government loaned the companies
  $61 million.
• Despite this, both companies nearly went bust!
  This was mainly because of the difficulty of
  building the railroad.
• The Pacific Railroad Act also set up the first
  transcontinental electric telegraph. This ran
  alongside the track of the railroad.
```

Figure 2.5 A fact file on the first Transcontinental Railroad.

The railroads and settlement of the West

The railroad companies used marketing to encourage settlers to buy their land. They laid on special trips to show people the attractions of the area. The railway companies also organised loans to help people buy the land, and sent successful settlers on tours to recruit new customers.

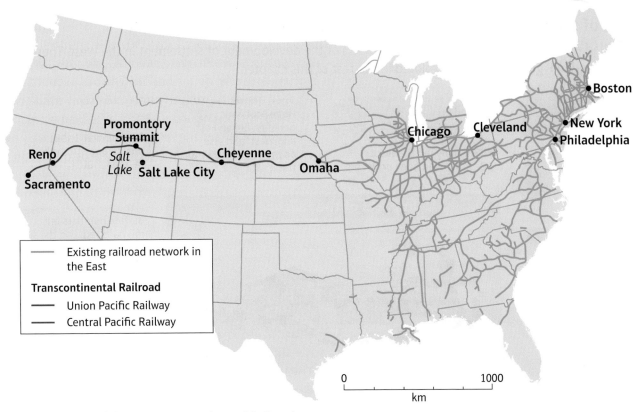

Figure 2.2 The route of the First Transcontinental Railroad.

Each railroad company had a Bureau of Immigration to persuade people from foreign countries to settle on the Plains. One railroad agent said he persuaded 10,000 Scandinavians to settle in Nebraska.

By 1880, the railroad companies had settled 200 million acres in the West. The railroad companies turned out to be more important than the Homestead Act in encouraging settlement. This was because they had more land to sell, better marketing and because people wanted to settle near the railroad.

Source B

An 1872 advert for land for sale by the Burlington & Missouri River Railroad Company.

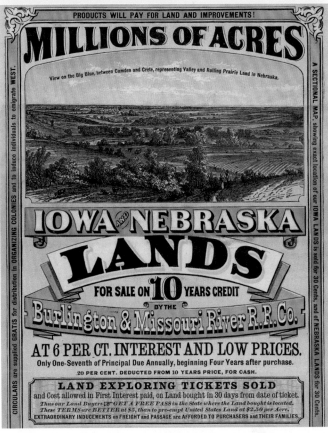

Activities ?

1 You are working for a railroad company's advertising department. Design a poster to encourage poor farmers from Europe to come and settle on a homestead on the Plains.

2 The number of migrants using the Oregon Trail fell sharply after 1869. Explain how this was connected to the First Transcontinental Railroad.

43

Impacts of the railroads

Railroads had major impacts on many different aspects of the development of settlement in the West. These impacts are summarised in Figure 2.3 and are explored in the rest of this chapter.

Made travelling west much easier

Encouraged immigration from Europe

Towns grew rapidly along railroad routes

Farmers could transport their crops to sell in the big cities

Settlers could buy products from industrial cities (agricultural machinery, clothes, household items, etc.)

Linked up western territories with the East and made them a part of the USA. Many felt 'Manifest Destiny*' had been achieved

Huge economic benefits: linked East and West, and also opened up the USA to trade with Asia

Plains Indian tribes moved away from the railroad routes

Buffalo numbers fell: railroads reduced the size of grasslands and brought hunters to the Plains

Plains Indian attacks on railroad workers led to conflict with the US Army

Railroads led the way for the invasion of Plains Indians' lands by white Americans

Enabled growth of the cattle industry: Texas cattlemen could transport and sell cattle to the cities

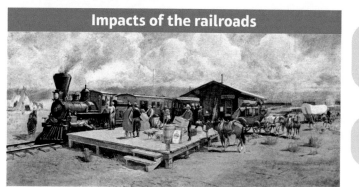

Impacts of the railroads

Impacts on settlers and farming Impacts on the Plains Indians National impacts Impacts on the cattle industry

Figure 2.3 Major impacts of the railroads on the development of settlement in the West.

Tackling the problems of homesteading

The railroad companies did not tell people they were selling land to about the problems of farming the Plains.

Homesteading on the Plains was very hard (see pages 24–26). Homesteaders needed savings of between $800 and $1,000 to: plough fields, dig a well, buy horses and farming equipment, and build a house and outbuildings. If there was little rain then no crops could be grown to sell and homesteaders could quickly run out of money.

Key term

Manifest Destiny*

The belief that it was God's will for white people to take possession of the whole of the USA and make it productive and civilised.

The effects of the railroads

The railroad did make homestead life easier as:

- homesteaders could visit family members much more easily, which lessened the loneliness of homestead life

- homesteaders could order manufactured products that made life easier (like farming equipment or new clothes) which were delivered to the nearest railroad station

- towns sprang up along the railroads, which gave homesteaders a place to meet, socialise and share news and ideas.

These improvements to homesteader life meant that more homesteaders came to the Plains to settle.

New inventions

The table below shows three important inventions that helped make farming the Plains easier.

As new inventions were shown to be of use to farmers and became cheaper to buy, they began to be used all across the West. Before 1876, however, they were still 'in development' and were not widely used (see Chapter 3).

	1854: 'self-governing' windmill, 1870 steel blades	1874: barbed wire	1875: sulky plow
Purpose	Windmills were used to pump water out of the ground to help farmers water their crops.	Barbed wire was used to fence off crops to protect them from livestock and other animals.	Strong ploughs were needed to plough up the tough weeds and prairie grass on the Great Plains.
Advantage	Halladay's windmill (or wind pump) could pump water out of quite deep wells (30 feet). From 1870, steel blades meant the windmills could stand up better to strong winds.	Very effective and much cheaper than buying timber for fences.	The 'sulky plow' was a very strong, easy-to-operate steel plough that made ploughing up tough plants much easier. 50,000 sulky plows were sold in the first six years of production.
Problems	Not powerful enough to pump up water from very deep wells (more than 30 feet) and needed constant maintenance. It was not until the 1880s that these problems were overcome: see page 72.	Not widely used until after 1880. Early types broke and rusted.	Six times as many basic ploughs were sold in the same period – these were cheaper. Early sulkies were unstable and could tip up.

Extend your knowledge

Barbed wire

Barbed wire was used a lot in the West. Laws required farmed land to be separated from roaming cattle by fences. Laws also stated that railroad companies were responsible for any accidents on their lines if tracks had not been fenced off. Joseph Glidden, the 'Father of Barbed Wire', became a millionaire.

Activity ?

For each one of the three inventions shown here, identify the problem of farming in the West that they were designed to overcome. Look back at pages 24–26 for the problems.

New crops

In 1873, a Russian religious community called the Mennonites moved to the Great Plains. Mennonites discovered that 'Turkey Red' wheat grew well on their Kansas farms. Soon farmers with good land were able to export* grain, which encouraged more farmers to settle on the Plains.

The Timber Culture Act (1873)

The **Timber Culture Act** allowed a homesteader to claim another 160 acres if she or he promised to plant trees on a quarter of it. Trees were important because they could:

- act as a 'wind break': slow down the Great Plains winds to shelter crops from damage
- provide settlers with timber for building houses, fences and furniture, and for repairing equipment
- provide settlers with wood to burn to keep warm.

The Timber Culture Act aimed to reduce the high rate of failure of homesteads in the Great Plains. 16 million acres were claimed under the Timber Culture Act by 1878. Unfortunately most of the trees planted died because there was not enough water for them. Only in the state of Minnesota did the trees grow well.

People used the Timber Culture Act to claim land that they did not plan to settle on. After waiting for a few years for the price of land to rise, they sold their claims for a profit. The Act was heavily criticised for this.

Key terms
Export*
Selling and sending products to other countries .
Lawless*
Where laws are not enforced and people can do what they like because there is nobody to stop them.

Problems of law and order
Impact of the railroads – 'Hell on Wheels'

The new towns created by the railroads were lawless* places at first – they were known as '**Hell on Wheels**'. The most lawless railroad towns of all were the 'cow towns'. After long weeks herding cattle to these towns, cowboys would load the cows onto railroad wagons and then be paid their wages. The cowboys would then go out celebrating, which could lead to trouble. The town of **Abilene** in Kansas is a good example of the problems of new railroad towns.

Abilene was a cow town in Kansas. When the railroad reached Kansas in 1867, the town's population went up from 500 to 7,000 people.

↓

Lawlessness got out of control: there was gunfighting and murders, gambling, prostitution and drunkenness.

↓

The townspeople built a jail in 1870. The cowboys tore it down.

↓

A town marshal was hired in 1870 who banned guns. This was quite successful at first, but he was murdered with an axe in November 1870.

↓

In April 1871, 'Wild Bill' Hickok was hired as town marshal. He spent all his time gambling.

↓

At the end of 1871, Hickok was sacked. Abilene banned cowboys – even though that meant an end to the cattle trade in Abilene.

Figure: Lawlessness in Abilene, Kansas, 1867–71.

Impact of the Civil War

The Civil War (1861–65) increased the likelihood of trouble in the West. This was because of army deserters* and because of the arrival of large numbers of ex-soldiers in the West after the war.

These ex-soldiers sometimes formed dangerous gangs of outlaws that were difficult for law enforcement to control.

Key terms

Deserters*

Soldiers who run away from the army. Deserting was a criminal offence.

Vigilance committee*

Townspeople who got together to organise their own law enforcement.

Lynched*

Killed by a group of ordinary people without a proper trial.

The Reno Gang

The Reno Gang were a group of Civil War deserters, con-men and thieves.

In 1866, the Reno Gang carried out a train robbery stealing $16,000. The owners of the money hired detectives from the Pinkerton National Detective Agency to hunt down the gang. The detectives caught John Reno, but the gang kept going. Their fourth train robbery got them $96,000.

The next time they robbed a train, one of the gang was captured. He gave up the rest of the gang in return for a reduced sentence. However, when the gang was arrested, a vigilance committee* arrived. The committee took all the gang members away from the Pinkertons, and lynched* them.

Source C

A photo showing Pinkerton agents. The man sitting down is the son of Alfred Pinkerton, who founded Pinkerton's National Detective Agency in 1850.

Lawlessness and the West

The rapidly growing population, and the Civil War, meant that local communities became unable to enforce the law themselves and the state or federal government did not have the resources to help.

Victims of lawlessness had to meet force with force, either by hiring a tough sheriff or town marshal to keep the peace, or by hiring a private police force, like the Pinkertons.

However, most places in the West were not lawless. Even in the wildest cow towns, murders were rare. Stealing was common, because so may people were struggling to survive. But because no one could afford to lose property in this way, local communities tried hard to catch and punish thieves.

THINKING HISTORICALLY | Cause and Consequence (2c)

Far-reaching consequences

The American Civil War (1861–65) was an important event in the history of the West. It had consequences in several different areas.

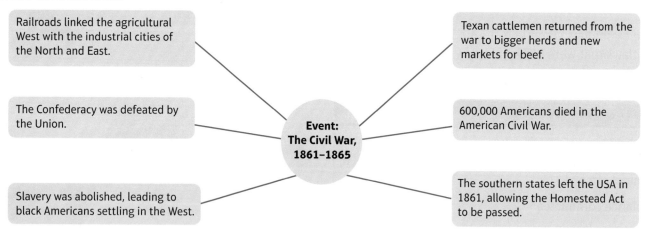

Railroads linked the agricultural West with the industrial cities of the North and East.

Texan cattlemen returned from the war to bigger herds and new markets for beef.

The Confederacy was defeated by the Union.

600,000 Americans died in the American Civil War.

Event: The Civil War, 1861–1865

Slavery was abolished, leading to black Americans settling in the West.

The southern states left the USA in 1861, allowing the Homestead Act to be passed.

1 How many consequences have been identified? Have any consequences mentioned in this section been missed?

2 Suggest a category (e.g. political, social, cultural, economic) for each consequence.

3 Explain why the Pacific Railroad Act was a consequence of the Civil War.

4 If a historian was writing about the history of the Great Plains, which consequences might they leave out?

Summary

- New settlers arrived in the West following the Civil War, helped by the government's Homestead Act (1862) and Pacific Railroad Act (1862), and by the railroad companies.
- The new settlers started to benefit from new methods of farming the Plains.
- The new settlement following the Civil War and the building of railroads into the West brought new problems of law and order to some areas.

Checkpoint

Strengthen

S1 Explain the importance of the Pacific Railroad Act (1862) for the settlement of the West.

S2 Identify the connections between: a) the Civil War b) the railroads c) problems of law and order in the West.

Challenge

C1 Study Figure 2.1 at the start of this chapter. Write a sentence to explain the importance of each box in the diagram to the development of settlement in the West.

How confident do you feel about your answers to these questions? Continuing your American West timeline will help: now you can start to add some key events for the period 1862–76.

2.2 Ranching and the cattle industry

Learning outcomes

- Understand the growth of the cattle industry after the Civil War.
- Understand the significance of this growth, including the effects on cowboys and the rivalry between ranchers and homesteaders.

In the 1870s, settlers were spreading westwards along the railroad to states and territories* in the West. Prospectors were also spreading eastwards through the Rocky Mountains looking for gold. The growth of the cattle industry in Texas also spread people and settlements from the South.

Timeline

The growth of the cattle industry

1836 Start of Texan cattle drives to Missouri (Shawnee Trail)

1855 Quarantine law in Missouri blocks Texas cattle

1861 Iliff buys a herd of cows and fattens them on the Plains in Colorado Territory

1861–65 The American Civil War – longhorn cattle numbers boom

1866 Kansas farmers stop a drive from Texas to Sedalia, Missouri

1866 Goodnight and Loving drive cattle to Fort Sumner, New Mexico

1867 McCoy sets up the first cow town, Abilene, Kansas

1868 Goodnight–Loving Trail lengthened to Cheyenne, Wyoming

1870 Iliff's ranch increases in size to 16,000 acres of open range

1867–72 A total of three million cattle driven along the Chisholm Trail to Abilene

The Texan cattle industry before the Civil War

1836: Texas became independent from Mexico and the Texan cattle industry began. Texans learned cowboy skills from Mexican cattle herders.

↓

Texan cowboys herded their cattle on long drives* along cattle trails* across the South, or up to towns in Missouri to sell them.

↓

From Missouri, the cows went by rail to big cities in the North and East.

↓

Some Texan cows carried a deadly disease called 'Texas fever'. They often infected cows in Missouri and Kansas on the long drives.

↓

1855: Missouri formed vigilance committees to block the cattle drives.

↓

1859: Missouri and Kansas passed quarantine* laws saying that no Texan cattle were allowed into their states.

Figure: The Texan cattle industry, 1836–59.

Key terms

Territory*

When the population of an area in the West reached 5,000 settlers, it became a territory. (When the population reached 60,000, it became a state.)

Long drives*

Herding cattle (or other animals) over long distances.

Cattle trails*

Routes used for driving cattle: these needed to have easy access to both grass and water.

Quarantine*

Keeping an animal that might be diseased away from other animals to stop the spread of disease.

Growth of the cattle industry after the war

After the Civil War ended in 1865, beef was in great demand in the big industrial cities of the North.

- In 1865 a cow was worth $40 in Chicago.
- But the economy of the South had been damaged by the war and people couldn't afford beef: a cow was only worth $5 in Texas.
- Longhorns (a breed of cattle) in Texas had been left unmanaged during the war and their numbers had increased enormously: there were five million cows in Texas in 1865.

In 1866, to cash in on this extra money in the North, Texans organised a large cattle drive to Sedalia, but they were stopped from crossing through Kansas by farmers worried that the Texan cows would spread Texas fever.

The significance of Joseph McCoy and Abilene

In 1867, a branch line of the railroad reached Abilene, Kansas. A Chicago livestock trader called Joseph McCoy realised that Abilene could be a new end point for cattle drives. It had three key advantages.

In 1867, Kansas changed the quarantine rule so that it was no longer so strict. Texan cattle could now be driven through the state if they kept to the west of where farmers had settled. Abilene was in this western zone.

Figure 2.10 The advantages of Abilene as an end point for cattle drives.

There was grassland all the way from Kansas, through Indian Territory, to Texas. There was a trade route through this grassland called the **Chisholm Trail** that cowboys could use to bring the herds north.

Cattle could be loaded onto railroad trucks (boxcars) at the railhead at Abilene and shipped from there to Chicago.

Source A

Texas Longhorn cattle being loaded into a railroad boxcar in Abilene, from *Leslie's Illustrated Newspaper*, 1871.

What did McCoy do?

1 He bought 450 acres of land near Abilene and built pens for keeping cows.

2 He persuaded the railroad company to build a large depot where cattle could be loaded onto trains.

3 He built a hotel in Abilene.

4 He had the Chisholm Trail marked out properly and extended so that it ended in Abilene.

5 He spent $5,000 marketing Abilene to Texan cattlemen, highlighting the good trail, new facilities and large profits to be made.

Three million cows were driven to Abilene between 1867 and 1872. Abilene expanded and became a famous 'cow town'. McCoy became very rich.

The significance of the Goodnight–Loving Trail

The **Goodnight–Loving Trail** was set up in 1866 by Charles Goodnight and Oliver Loving. They realised there was an opportunity to sell cattle directly to new population centres in the West.

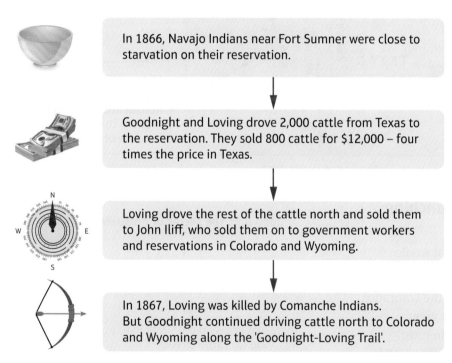

In 1866, Navajo Indians near Fort Sumner were close to starvation on their reservation.

Goodnight and Loving drove 2,000 cattle from Texas to the reservation. They sold 800 cattle for $12,000 – four times the price in Texas.

Loving drove the rest of the cattle north and sold them to John Iliff, who sold them on to government workers and reservations in Colorado and Wyoming.

In 1867, Loving was killed by Comanche Indians. But Goodnight continued driving cattle north to Colorado and Wyoming along the 'Goodnight-Loving Trail'.

Figure: The Goodnight–Loving Cattle Trail.

By 1876, Goodnight was so successful that his ranch* in Texas covered one million acres. Other cattle drivers started to use the trail to Wyoming, too. As a result, Wyoming began to develop its own cattle industry (see page 83 for consequences).

Key term

Ranch*
A large farm for breeding and keeping cattle, rather than for crops.

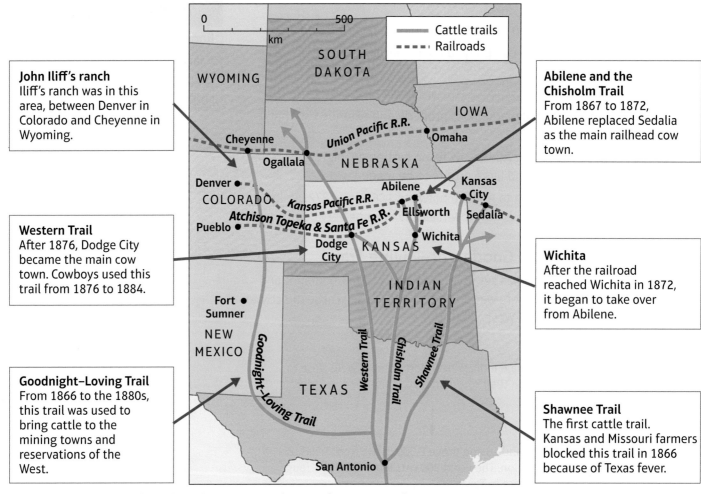

John Iliff's ranch
Iliff's ranch was in this area, between Denver in Colorado and Cheyenne in Wyoming.

Abilene and the Chisholm Trail
From 1867 to 1872, Abilene replaced Sedalia as the main railhead cow town.

Western Trail
After 1876, Dodge City became the main cow town. Cowboys used this trail from 1876 to 1884.

Wichita
After the railroad reached Wichita in 1872, it began to take over from Abilene.

Goodnight–Loving Trail
From 1866 to the 1880s, this trail was used to bring cattle to the mining towns and reservations of the West.

Shawnee Trail
The first cattle trail. Kansas and Missouri farmers blocked this trail in 1866 because of Texas fever.

Figure 2.4 The main cattle trails and cow towns in the West from 1866 to the 1880s.

John Iliff and the beginnings of ranching on the Plains

In 1861, John Iliff spotted an opportunity that would bring significant changes to the cattle industry.

In the same year, a gold rush had started in the Colorado Rocky Mountains. This meant that there was great demand for meat. However, Denver (the main town) had no railroad link (until 1870) and it was difficult and expensive to transport supplies there.

Iliff bought a cheap herd of cows that had been driven up from Texas. He realised that if he could fatten his new herd up on the grass of the Plains, he would be able to sell beef for a good price to the mining towns with none of the expense and difficulty of the long drives.

By 1870, Iliff had built up a huge herd on the Colorado Plains: 26,000 cattle. He became Denver's first millionaire, selling beef to the mining towns, to the teams building the Union Pacific Railroad, and to the government for Plains Indian reservations.

John Iliff: the secret of his success

⬇

Miners in the Colorado Rockies wanted meat. but there was no railway to bring in supplies.

⬇

There was grass on the Great Plains that was good for cattle to eat.

⬇

Instead of driving cows up from Texas, he reared them on the Colorado Plains.

Figure: Why John Iliff became a successful rancher.

This was the start of a new phase in the cattle industry: ranching on the open range* of the Great Plains.

Source B

Extract from an obituary of 23 February 1878 in *The Denver Times* for John Iliff, 'The Cattle King of Colorado', following his death.

He went to work with a will [he worked very hard], gave almost his entire time and generally a great share of his personal attention to his herds. He saw them grow, knew where they ranged [where the cows wandered to], understood when it was a good time to buy and a good time to sell; indeed he gave his business that untiring attention that never fails to find its reward in the gains [profits] that follow. His life was a worthy example to other men, and is a fair illustration of what may be accomplished by well directed effort on the plains of the Far West.

The cattle barons

The 1870s saw a 'beef bonanza' in the West. The big growth was in ranching on the Plains. Through the 1870s, the cattle industry was seen as a sure way to make money. As a result, people invested* huge amounts of money in the industry.

The best way to make a lot of money was to have very large ranches and enormous herds of cattle. A few men, backed by rich investors, controlled the cattle industry. They were called the **cattle barons** because of their wealth and influence.

Interpretation 1

From *The Great American Desert* (1966) by W. E. Hollon. Here he describes how the right conditions came about to cause the rapid growth of the cattle industry.

Suddenly, the right conditions fell into place... the Civil War brought an increased demand for beef... settlers learned that cattle could thrive on the native grass and survive the drastic changes in climate; the transcontinental railroads pushed to the Pacific... .

Key terms

Open range*

A large area of unfenced land over which livestock roamed freely.

Invested*

To put money into a business in order to receive more money back if the business becomes successful.

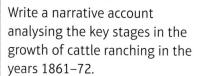

Exam-style question, Section A

Write a narrative account analysing the key stages in the growth of cattle ranching in the years 1861–72.

You may use the following in your answer:

- Joseph McCoy and Abilene
- cattle barons.

You **must** also use information of your own.   **8 marks**

Exam tip

Try to include at least three key stages. Start with the situation in 1861.

- The Texas cattle industry was struggling in 1861 because Texan cattle could not be driven through Missouri or Kansas because of…

Then move onto the end of the Civil War (1865):

- After the war, there was high demand for beef in the big cities of the North. Joseph McCoy realised that…
- At around the same time, John Iliff spotted another opportunity: the rapidly-growing mining towns of the Rocky Mountains. He realised that…

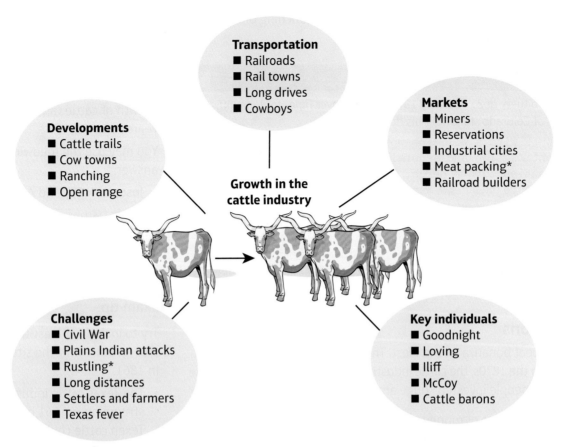

Figure 2.5 Factors affecting the growth of the cattle industry before and after the Civil War.

Activity ?

Using Figure 2.5 to help you:

a explain how key individuals found new ways to make money from selling cattle after the Civil War

b explain how cow towns were connected to the growth of the cattle industry

c identify as many connections as you can between railroads and the growth in the cattle industry from 1862 to 1876.

Key terms

Meat packing*

Slaughtering, processing and packing of meat for distribution around the country.

Rustling*

Stealing livestock.

Cowboys and changes in the cattle industry

Life on the long drive

Driving a herd of cows from Texas to Kansas up the Chisholm Trail took between two and three months. Herding cattle up the Goodnight–Loving Trail to Cheyenne could take six months. It was hard work.

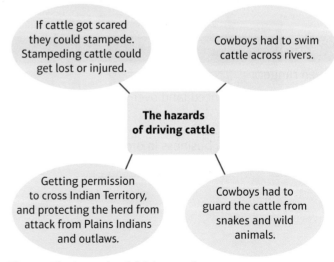

Figure: The hazards of driving cattle.

Source C

A coloured engraving from the early 1870s depicting cowboys driving cattle up the Chisholm Trail. Note the long line of cattle with cowboys spaced out along it.

There were often up to 3,000 cattle on a long drive.

3,000 cattle needed an **outfit** of around 12 cowboys to manage.

The cowboys were led by a **trail boss** who decided how fast to go and where to camp.

Trail bosses were paid around $100 a month for a long drive. Cowboys got $20–$30 a month.

The outfit always had a **chuck wagon**. This carried the food, water, equipment and a cook.

The outfit also had a **wrangler** who looked after the horses.

Cowboys slept in the open, taking it in turns to guard the herd.

The herd was organised into a long line with cowboys at the front, middle and end.

The herd would travel around 15 or 20 miles a day.

- At the end of the trail, the cowboys would herd the cattle into the stockyards (enclosed pens).
- Once the cattle were sold, the cowboys would move the cattle onto trains.
- Then the outfit was paid.
- Once they had been paid, cowboys would celebrate by drinking, dancing and – often – fighting.
- Cowboys often spent all their money in town and would then borrow money to get back to Texas for the next drive the following spring.

Life on the ranch

Cattle in Texas were raised on ranches, which often covered huge areas of open land. Through the winter, the cattle roamed freely, mixing together with cattle from other ranches.

During the winter months, most ranches did not employ many cowboys. Cowboys often got a different job, such as working in a bar.

Cowboys who stayed on ranches over the winter spent their time repairing equipment, riding out to check on the animals, and planning the year ahead.

Extend your knowledge

Crossing Indian Territory

The Chisholm Trail went through Indian Territory. These tribes required payment from the cowboys in return for permission to cross their lands. Warriors patrolled the lands to make sure payments were collected. Conflicts sometimes occurred when trail bosses refused to pay.

The real ranch work began in early spring with the round-up.

- Teams of cowboys rode out from a central location on the range, then worked their way back in, driving ahead of them all the cattle they had found.
- When all the cattle were rounded up, cowboys began the work of separating them out. Cattle were branded to show which ranch they belonged to.

Source D

A 19th-century engraving of a round-up. It was unusual for older men to work as cowboys because it was such a tough, demanding way of life.

Life on the ranch was hard work: usually too hard for anyone much older than their early 20s. Older cowboys either found new jobs in towns, or set up ranches of their own.

On most ranches there was a bunkhouse where all the cowboys lived together. Bunkhouses were usually cold and draughty during the winter. There was not much entertainment and often there were strict rules. For example, Charles Goodnight banned gambling on his ranches. Once or twice a year there were dances at local towns, which was the highpoint of the ranch's social life.

Ranches on the Plains
Similarities

Ranches on the Plains were open range and they carried out spring round-ups in just the same way as in Texas. Cowboys still needed to drive the herds over the Plains from the ranch to the railhead: but the drives were much shorter and took days rather than months.

Differences

- Winter was harder on the Plains. If snow and ice was too deep, the cattle could not get to the grass underneath.
- Cowboys would have to ride out during blizzards to find the herds and make sure they had shelter, food and water to drink.
- On the biggest ranches, cowboys would be sent out over the winter to stay in cabins around the ranch. Sometimes these cowboys spent the winter on their own.

Activities ?

1. Compare the life of cowboys who went on long drives with the lives of cowboys who lived on ranches. Identify at least one similarity and one difference.
2. Write a letter home from a teenage cowboy who has just completed his first spring round-up. Describe the challenges of the job and what the cowboy enjoyed and did not enjoy.
3. Describe three ways in which ranching on the Plains meant changes in the life of cowboys.

Rivalry between ranchers and homesteaders

Ranching on the open range needed a lot of land – at least 2,000 acres and usually much more. The ranchers did not buy all this land as that would have been very expensive. Instead, they made use of public land. Federal* law said that everyone was able to pasture livestock on public land. Ranchers divided up the range between themselves.

When homesteading spread to ranching country, it threatened ranching. Ranchers used many different tactics to block homesteading on 'their' public land.

- Ranchers would file claims under the Homestead Act themselves for the bits of land on the ranch that contained waterholes or springs. No farmer would want the rest of the land, with no access to water.

- Ranch-hands and family members would file Homestead Act claims to parcels of land throughout the ranch area and then hand those rights over to the ranch owner.

- Rich ranchers took homesteaders to court over claims. Most homesteaders did not have the money to pay lawyers and court costs and so would have to give up their claims.

- Some ranchers also threatened homesteaders with violence, damaged their crops and accused them of rustling cows from the ranch's herd.

Key term

Federal*

Each US state has its own state government. There is also the federal government which governs over all the states. Laws made by the federal government apply to all states.

Ranchers	v.	Homesteaders

Ranchers

Ranching relied on access to huge amounts of **public** grazing land.

Ranchers used legal and illegal tactics to block homesteaders from claiming public land that ranching relied on.

Ranchers complained that homesteaders' barbed wire fences hurt their cattle. They also accused homesteaders of stealing their cows.

Homesteaders

Homesteading turned small parcels of public land into **private** farms.

Homesteaders accused ranchers of letting their cows graze on their crops. They said ranchers should put up fences to stop this happening. Ranchers said it was homesteaders' responsibility to fence off their land.

Figure 2.6 The rivalry between ranchers and homesteaders.

Tensions between homesteaders and ranchers sometimes led to open conflicts, known as range wars. The most famous range war was the Johnson County War (see page 83).

Conflicts over sheep farming

There were also conflicts between cattlemen and sheepherders. Large-scale sheep farming started in the 1870s in the West, for example in Wyoming. Violent clashes between cattle ranchers and sheepherders resulted in several deaths in the 1870s.

Cattle ranchers said sheep damaged the grass, leaving nothing for the cows.

Cattle ranchers fenced off grazing land to stop sheep using it.

Conflicts between cattlemen and sheepherders

Cattle ranchers said sheep spread a disease, called 'sheep scab'.

Sheepherders cut fences to allow sheep to graze.

Figure: Why did cattlemen and sheepherders come into conflict?

Exam-style question, Section A

Explain **two** consequences of the development of ranching on the Plains in the years 1866–76. **8 marks**

Exam tip

Remember to include **two** consequences in your answer and spend equal time on both.

Summary

- The period from 1862 to 1876 saw rapid growth of the cattle industry, including the development of ranching on the Great Plains.
- Goodnight, Iliff and McCoy introduced new ways to meet growing demand for beef in both eastern and western USA, all of which had important consequences for the cattle industry.
- Cowboys on long drives had very different lives from when they worked on ranches. There were both freedoms and dangers on the long drive.
- As homesteaders began to claim the public land that the ranchers depended on, the two groups began to clash.

Checkpoint

Strengthen

S1 Explain why the town of Abilene was important for the cattle industry.

S2 Describe the ways in which McCoy, Goodnight and Iliff changed the cattle industry.

S3 Why did the use of public land become a cause of conflict between ranchers and homesteaders?

Challenge

C1 Explain how the development of railroads across the West influenced the growth of the cattle industry.

How confident do you feel about your answers to these questions? Figure 2.5 (page 54) groups together some of the key factors and events in the growth of the cattle industry in this period. It could help you to think through the ways these key factors and events linked up.

2.3 Changes in the way of life of the Plains Indians

The expansion of the railroad, the growing cattle industry and gold prospecting all increased the pressures on the Plains Indians' traditional way of life.

The impact of railroads

By signing the Fort Laramie Treaty (1851), Plains Indian tribes agreed to let railroad surveyors and construction teams enter their lands. But when they signed the treaty, the tribes did not know that allowing railroads to cross their land also meant:

- land grants along the railroad to white settlers
- hunters travelling by train to hunt buffalo.

> **Buffalo migration routes were blocked** because railroad companies had to fence off parts of the railroad.

> **Plains Indians lost land** because the US government gave land along the tracks to railroad companies which sold the land to white settlers.

> **Impacts of the railroads on the Plains Indians' way of life**

> **Buffalo were exterminated** (all were killed) because hunters travelled by train to kill thousands of them.

> **Plains Indians were moved to reservations*** – the US government persuaded them to move to reservations away from railroad routes.

Figure: Impacts of the railroads.

Key term

Reservation*

An area of land 'reserved' for use by American Indians and managed by the US government.

Source A

An 1868 engraving of Plains Indians attacking a train along the Union Pacific Railroad.

The cattle industry

Cattle and buffalo both ate grass. As a result, as cattle numbers increased on the Plains, buffalo numbers declined.

- In 1860, there were 130,000 cattle in the West, all in Kansas and Nebraska.
- In 1880, there were 4.5 million cattle: half of those were in Colorado, Wyoming, Montana and Dakota.

As buffalo became hard to find, some Plains Indians went to work as cowboys or on ranches. Ranching took Plains Indians away from traditional lifestyles. It meant they worked for money and depended on ranchers for a job.

Activities ?

1 Name three pressures on the Plains Indians that increased tensions between tribes and white Americans.

2 Produce your own diagram, similar to Figure 2.7 (you could use photos or your own drawings). Expand the captions for each picture to explain, in your own words, why each item led to increased tension or how it resulted from conflict between white Americans and Plains Indians.

Cattle trails also affected Plains Indians, who patrolled to see who was using the trails. Some tribes, especially the Comanche, attacked cowboys and stole horses and cattle from long drives. This resulted in the US Army riding out to attack the tribes.

Gold prospecting

Of all the threats to American Indian ways of life, gold prospecting was the most catastrophic because the changes it brought happened so rapidly.

- In California, gold prospectors had murdered American Indians to get them away from possible claims to gold.
- Men coming to California from all over the world brought new diseases that devastated American Indian populations.
- New towns developed, with churches, schools and stores, which were very different to American Indian culture.

In 1862, gold was discovered in Montana Territory. The quickest route from the East to the mining area was through the Lakota Sioux's hunting grounds. Thousands travelled along this route, called the **Bozeman Trail**, despite this being against the terms of the Fort Laramie Treaty (see page 28). Red Cloud's War (see page 65) was a direct consequence of these tensions.

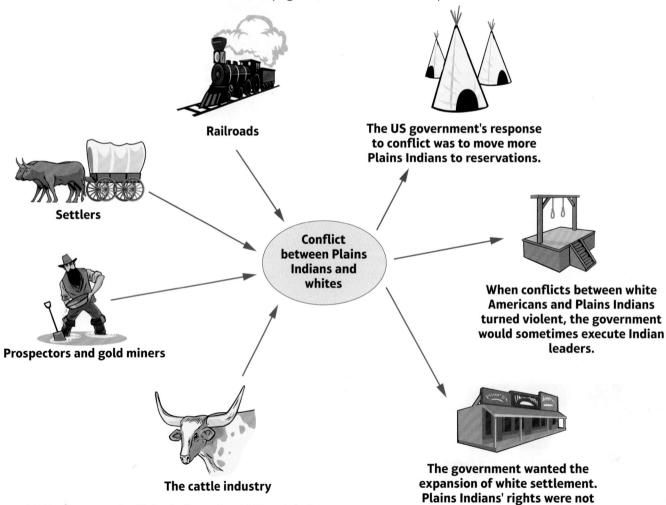

Railroads

Settlers

Prospectors and gold miners

The cattle industry

Conflict between Plains Indians and whites

The US government's response to conflict was to move more Plains Indians to reservations.

When conflicts between white Americans and Plains Indians turned violent, the government would sometimes execute Indian leaders.

The government wanted the expansion of white settlement. Plains Indians' rights were not allowed to stop this happening.

Figure 2.7 Pressures on the Plains Indians after 1862 and their consequences.

US government policy towards Plains Indians and its impacts

As more white Americans moved onto the Plains the government continued its policy of moving Plains Indians onto reservations. In return, the US government said that the Plains Indians would:

- not lose any more land
- be protected from attack by white Americans
- be given yearly payments (in money but also in food, livestock, clothing and farming equipment).

Why did Plains Indians move to reservations?

- Because tribal councils thought there was no other way for the tribe to survive as white American settlement expanded and food became scarce.
- Because the US government promised to protect the tribe on its reservation, and provide food regularly – as well as allowing the tribe to continue hunting.

Once it became clear that the government did not keep these promises, other tribes either refused to move onto reservations, or would not stay on them. The US Army was used to force Plains Indians to move to reservations or return to them if they left.

Impacts of the reservations

There were major problems with reservations that had serious and negative impacts on Plains Indian people.

- **The reservations showed no understanding of Plains Indian culture.** Treaties about reservations were agreed with chiefs, but chiefs could not make bands or brotherhoods stay on the reservation. Reservations were sometimes a long way from the tribe's sacred places. Traditional enemies were sometimes placed on the same reservation (e.g. Apache and Navajo).

American Indian homelands and reservations 1862

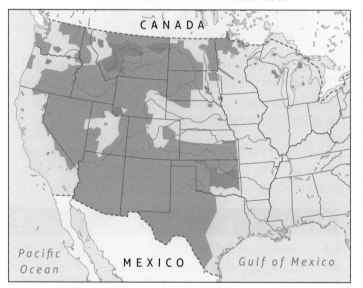

American Indian homelands and reservations 1876

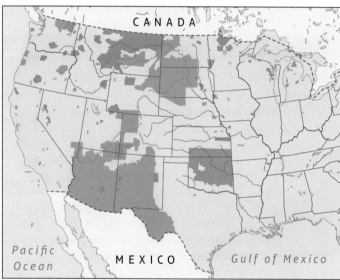

Reservation
American Indian homelands

Figure 2.8 Changes in American Indian lands between 1862 and 1876. The blue areas are homelands where American Indians continued to live freely. The red areas are reservations.

- **Poor farming land.** The US government wanted Plains Indians to learn farming. But the reservations often had very poor farming land (that whites did not want) and some tribes had no traditions of farming at all. When crops failed, the Plains Indians had to be given food by the government.
- **Corruption and cheating.** The management of reservations was the responsibility of the Bureau of Indian Affairs. It appointed agents who ran each reservation. These men were often corrupt and cheated the tribes in order to make themselves wealthy.
- **Reducing the size of reservations.** White settlers were angry at the size of some reservations and complained that the Plains Indians were being treated better than they were. The government used any excuse to reduce the size of reservations.

President Grant's 'Peace Policy' (1868)

Problems on the reservations led directly to conflicts between the Plains Indians and the US Army. In 1868, President Ulysses S. Grant put forward a '**Peace Policy**'. This aimed to calm tensions by improving the management of the reservations.

Source B

From President Grant's State of the Union speech, 6 December 1869.

The building of railroads, and the access thereby given to all the agricultural and mineral regions of the country, is rapidly bringing civilized settlements into contact with all the tribes of Indians. No matter what ought to be the relations between such settlements and the [Indians], the fact is they do not harmonize well [they do not get on together], and one or the other has to give way in the end. A system which looks to the extinction of a race is too horrible for a nation to adopt... I see no substitute for such a system, except in placing all the Indians on large reservations, as rapidly as it can be done, and giving them absolute protection there.

The policy replaced corrupt reservation agents with religious men, who were meant to be fairer. Grant also appointed an American Indian, Ely Parker, as the Commissioner of Indian Affairs.

Money was provided to improve conditions on existing reservations and set up new reservations for tribes still living free.

Plains Indians who refused to go to the reservations would be attacked by the army.

Ely Parker argued that Plains Indians should be treated as 'helpless and ignorant wards' (a ward is a child that is put under the protection of an adult guardian). The government should decide what was best for its Plains Indian 'wards'.

Source C

This engraving of Ely S. Parker was made in 1866.

These views led to the **Indian Appropriation Act of 1871**. This said that the US government no longer had to agree treaties with tribes. Instead, the government could do what it thought was best for the tribes.

The Indian Appropriation Act (1871) therefore made it easier for the government to take land from the Plains Indians and give it to white American settlers.

Activities ?

1   Name three differences between life on the Plains Indian homelands and life on a reservation.
2   Look at Source B. What did President Grant think was the only solution to conflict between white settlement and the Plains Indians?
3   Working with a partner, describe two ways in which government policy towards the Plains Indians changed from 1834 to 1871.

Conflict with the Plains Indians

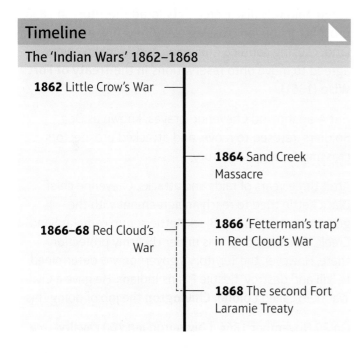

Timeline

The 'Indian Wars' 1862–1868

1862 Little Crow's War

1864 Sand Creek Massacre

1866–68 Red Cloud's War

1866 'Fetterman's trap' in Red Cloud's War

1868 The second Fort Laramie Treaty

Little Crow's War (1862)

Little Crow was a chief of a band of the Dakota Sioux in Minnesota. In 1850, there were 50,000 Plains Indians in Minnesota and only 6,000 whites. However, the number of white settlers was rapidly increasing, and the number of animals to hunt was rapidly declining.

In 1851, Dakota Sioux bands, including Little Crow's band, agreed to move to two reservations. Although the reservations were both small, Little Crow thought that the supplies and money the government promised would ensure the tribe's safety.

There were immediate problems with the treaty.

- The Dakota Sioux owed money to traders. The government refused to pay the Dakota Sioux their annuity* until these debts were paid off. But the Dakota Sioux weren't able to pay the traders back.

- The reservations could not produce enough food for the Dakota Sioux to survive on. When bands left the reservation to hunt, the reservation agent punished them by refusing to let them have their government supplies.

- The agent and local traders cheated the Dakota Sioux. The agent would hold onto annuity* payments until the starving Dakota Sioux agreed to very high prices for food.

- Settlers began to take pieces of reservation land along the Minnesota River that were good for farming.

- There was repeated trouble as warrior brotherhoods launched raids to capture resources, or broke into the agent's storehouses to steal supplies.

In 1858, the Dakota Sioux were made to sign away half of the reservation in return for money to pay the traders' debts. Little Crow said 'you promised us that we should have this same land forever, and yet now you want to take half of it away'.

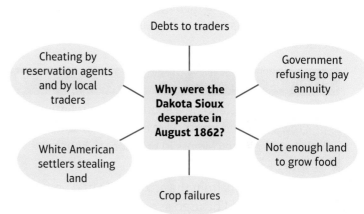

Figure: What went wrong for the Dakota Sioux.

By August 1862, the Dakota Sioux had no food or money. People tried to survive by eating grass.

The Civil War (1861–65) meant the US Army was busy. Little Crow and his band believed the time was right to take back what they felt was rightfully theirs.

- They took food from the agency's warehouses and shared it amongst their starving people.

- They then attacked the settlers' towns and army forts. Young Sioux warriors ignored their chiefs and slaughtered settlers, including women and children.

- In all, around 600 settlers and US soldiers were killed.

Key term

Annuity*

A payment made every year.

When government troops arrived, Little Crow and his followers fled into Dakota. Four hundred Dakota Sioux warriors were captured and put on trial. In the end, 38 of them were executed.

The rest of the Dakota Sioux in Minnesota were moved to the Crow Creek Reservation or to other reservations in Nebraska. Many of the Sioux starved to death on the Crow Creek Reservation that winter, because the land was so dry and poor. Bounties (reward money) were paid for killing any Dakota Sioux found hiding in Minnesota.

Little Crow himself had managed to make it back into Minnesota with his son, but he was shot by a hunter for the bounty money.

Activities

1   A director is planning a short film about Little Crow's War and wants a list of the main scenes. Identify the key events in the story to help her with her planning.

2   Identify points from the account of Little Crow's War that could be used as examples to support either of the following statements:

   a   The 'Peace Policy' of 1868 aimed to put right the bad management of some reservations.

   b   White American settlers viewed Plains Indians as little better than pests that needed to be exterminated.

The Sand Creek Massacre (1864)

When gold was discovered in Colorado Territory in 1858, prospectors began crossing over Cheyenne and Arapaho land, causing conflict. Cheyenne and Arapaho chiefs agreed to move onto reservations in the **Treaty of Fort Wise** (1861).

But Arapaho and Cheyenne braves, known as Dog Soldiers, refused to move, and attacked prospectors crossing Colorado Territory.

After three years of raids and attacks, Cheyenne chief Black Kettle tried to reach an agreement with the government and army. Black Kettle set up camp at Sand Creek. He believed he was under US Army protection there. However, the Territory's governor was determined to 'kill and destroy' hostile Plains Indians. He gave a Civil War hero called **Colonel Chivington** the job of doing this.

On 29 November 1864, Chivington led 700 cavalry troops on a dawn raid on Black Kettle's camp. Chivington claimed his troops fought a mighty battle against 1,000 warriors. This was not true. The camp put up a white flag of surrender, but Chivington and his men still massacred over 130 men, women, children and babies.

Source D

An engraving of the Sand Creek Massacre. This is a colour version of the original engraving, which was made in 1868.

Black Kettle escaped and carried news of the massacre to other tribes. The Dog Soldiers attacked forts and killed many white settlers across Colorado Territory.

The government was under great pressure in the Civil War and could not afford to send thousands of troops to Colorado to fight Plains Indians. Instead, a new treaty was agreed in 1865 to move the Cheyenne and Arapaho to a large new reservation.

However, once the Civil War was won, the US government backed out of the deal. Instead, in a treaty made in 1867:

- The Cheyenne and Arapaho were moved to a reservation half the size of what they had been promised in 1865.
- The compensation promised in 1865 was not paid to the survivors of the Sand Creek Massacre.

Red Cloud's War (1866–68)

Red Cloud was a respected war chief and warrior of the Lakota Sioux.

When gold was discovered in Montana in 1862, prospectors began to use a short cut off the Oregon Trail known as the Bozeman Trail. This trail crossed important Lakota Sioux hunting grounds and broke the terms of the Fort Laramie Treaty (1851). The Lakota Sioux began attacking the prospectors.

In 1866, the government called a council to discuss the conflict. Red Cloud was invited together with other Lakota Sioux chiefs.

Just before the council began, Red Cloud discovered that the army had already brought materials to build forts along the Bozeman Trail. He realised that the government was going to build forts and protect white settlers no matter what the Lakota Sioux agreed.

Red Cloud believed the Lakota Sioux must fight to protect their hunting grounds or starve.

Many bands followed Red Cloud in a two-year fight to prevent the Bozeman Trail from being used. They attacked soldiers and other workers building the forts. Red Cloud was joined by two other determined Lakota Sioux leaders, Sitting Bull and Crazy Horse (see page 10). Cheyenne and Arapaho bands also joined his war.

In total, Red Cloud's War may have involved nearly 3,000 Plains Indian warriors, fighting around 700 US soldiers.

Source E

A photograph (from 1891) showing Chief Red Cloud on the right of the picture, with another Lakota Sioux chief called American Horse, who is dressed in western clothing.

The Lakota Sioux used a tactic of deliberately getting spotted by US cavalry, then galloping off leading the pursuing cavalry into an ambush. In December 1866, Captain Fetterman and his 80 cavalry troops fell for this tactic. He and all his men were killed in what became known as **Fetterman's Trap**.

The Lakota Sioux surrounded Fort Phil Kearny, one of the forts on the Bozeman Trail. Troops could not leave the fort and no traveller could move along the Bozeman Trail. The government was forced to negotiate.

Figure: Red Cloud's War.

The second Fort Laramie Treaty (1868)

As a consequence of Red Cloud's success, the US government agreed to close the Bozeman Trail. In return, Red Cloud agreed to take his people to a reservation in Dakota. The second Fort Laramie Treaty recognised that this **Great Sioux Reservation** was only to be used by the Sioux nation. Not all of those who had fought with Red Cloud agreed with his signing the Treaty. Chief Sitting Bull and Crazy Horse were amongst those who refused to sign.

Activity ?

Why was Red Cloud able to achieve a victory for his people, while Black Kettle and Little Crow were not? Discuss this question as a class or in groups.

Source F

An extract from the 1868 Fort Laramie Treaty

The United States hereby agrees... that the country north of the North Platte river and east of the summits of the Big Horn mountains shall be held and considered to be... Indian territory, and also... that no white person or persons shall be permitted to settle upon or occupy any portion of [that land]; or without the consent of the Indians... to pass through [that land]; and it is further agreed by the United States, that within ninety days after the conclusion of peace with all the bands of the Sioux nation, the military posts now established in the territory... shall be abandoned, and that the road [the Bozeman Trail] leading to them and by them to the settlements in the Territory of Montana shall be closed.

Summary

- The white American invasion of Plains Indian lands caused major difficulties for the Plains Indians.
- Corrupt management of reservation food supplies led to desperation and then conflict.
- The US government continued to move Plains Indians to reservations.

Checkpoint

Strengthen

S1 Which tribes did Little Crow, Black Kettle and Red Cloud lead?

S2 Describe three causes of conflict between Plains Indians and white Americans.

Challenge

C1 What were the problems with President Grant's idea to integrate Native Americans into white American society? Write a paragraph to explain your thinking.

How confident do you feel about your answers to these questions? Figure 2.7 (page 60) models a way of representing factors and consequences of key events as a diagram. Try this approach for different topics.

Recap: Development of the Plains, c1862–c1876

Recall quiz

1 In what year did the American Civil War end – and who won?

2 How many acres were given to someone making a claim under the Homestead Act?

3 What were the names of the two companies set up by the Pacific Railroad Act?

4 In what year was the First Transcontinental Railroad completed?

5 What was invented in 1874 that made it much easier and cheaper for homesteaders to protect their crops and livestock?

6 What was the name of the trail that was used to drive cattle from Texas to Abilene?

7 Who introduced the first ranch on the Great Plains?

8 Describe one way in which cattle ranchers tried to stop homesteaders from settling on the public land used by their ranches.

9 What was the name of the trail that triggered Red Cloud's War?

10 Which US President introduced his 'Peace Policy' in 1868?

Exam-style question, Section A

Write a narrative account analysing the events of the Indian Wars, 1862–68.

You may use the following in your answer:

- Little Crow's War (1862)
- the second Fort Laramie Treaty (1868).

You **must** also use information of your own. **8 marks**

Exam tip

Include key events and make links between them to give an explained account. Make sure that you only cover the years given in the question and remember to add at least one of your own points.

Activities

1 Create three large timelines like the ones below. Decide which of the key events provided belongs to which timeline(s) and add them to the correct year on your timelines. The same event can appear on more than one timeline.

2 Which one event do you think was the most important for the settlement of the American West in the period from 1862 to 1876? Explain the choice you have made.

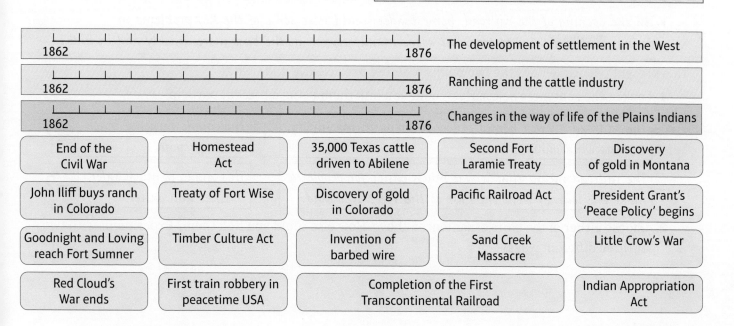

1862 — 1876	The development of settlement in the West
1862 — 1876	Ranching and the cattle industry
1862 — 1876	Changes in the way of life of the Plains Indians

End of the Civil War	Homestead Act	35,000 Texas cattle driven to Abilene	Second Fort Laramie Treaty	Discovery of gold in Montana
John Iliff buys ranch in Colorado	Treaty of Fort Wise	Discovery of gold in Colorado	Pacific Railroad Act	President Grant's 'Peace Policy' begins
Goodnight and Loving reach Fort Sumner	Timber Culture Act	Invention of barbed wire	Sand Creek Massacre	Little Crow's War
Red Cloud's War ends	First train robbery in peacetime USA	Completion of the First Transcontinental Railroad		Indian Appropriation Act

Writing historically: linking information

When you explain events and their consequences, you need to show how your ideas link together.

Learning outcomes

By the end of this lesson, you will understand how to:

- use present participles to link ideas clearly and concisely
- use other clauses to link ideas clearly and concisely.

Definitions

A present participle: ending in *-ing*, e.g. 'running', 'building', 'forming', 'falling', etc.

A past participle: often ending in *-ed*, e.g. 'formed', 'happened', etc. although there are several exceptions, e.g. 'ran', 'built', 'fell', etc.

An infinitive: the 'to' form of the verb, e.g. 'to run', 'to build', 'to form'.

How can I link ideas using present participles?

You can structure sentences to link related ideas in a number of different ways.

For example, look at all the different ways in which two sentences in the example answer below can be linked to this exam-style question:

> Explain **two** consequences of the opening of the First Transcontinental Railroad (1869). **(8 marks)**

With the opening of the railroad, homesteaders could solve some of the key problems in farming.	+	It enabled them to transport goods manufactured in the East more quickly and in bulk.	=

> With the opening of the railroad, homesteaders could solve some of the key problems in farming, enabling them to transport goods manufactured in the East more quickly and in bulk.

This present participle links the two points together very clearly and neatly.

1. Look at the sentences below. How could you link them using a present participle?

The railroad allowed homesteaders to bring in machinery, such as wind pumps.	+	This made farming much more efficient.	=?
The railroad meant that it was much easier for people to make the journey from the East to the West over land.	+	This made it much safer, quicker and easier.	=?

2. Choose **either** of the pairs of sentences above. How else could you link them? Experiment with two or three different ways.

Other ways to link ideas

There are two other ways to link ideas:

- **Infinitives** (e.g. 'to open', 'to make', 'to mean')
- **Past participles** (e.g. 'opened', 'made', 'meant')

Compare the sentences below, written in response to the exam-style question on the previous page:

> The First Transcontinental Railroad was opened in 1869. The railroad made a significant difference to the efficiency and productivity of farmers in the West.

This past participle allows the writer to connect these two points much more neatly.

> Opened in 1869, the First Transcontinental Railroad made a significant difference to the efficiency and productivity of farmers in the West.

Now compare these sentences, also written in response to the exam-style question on the previous page:

> Homesteaders could bring in barbed wire. This meant they could fence off and protect crops from cattle.

This infinitive allows the writer to link these two points much more neatly.

> Homesteaders could bring in barbed wire to fence off and protect crops from cattle.

3. How many of these points can you link using infinitives and past participles?

> Homesteaders could bring in wind pumps.
> These helped with watering the land.
> This made the land more fertile.

Did you notice?

Links can often be positioned at different points in a sentence without affecting its meaning. Experiment with one or two of the sentences above, trying the link in different positions.

Improving an answer

4. Look at the points noted below in response to this exam-style question:

> Explain the importance of cattle trails for the development of the cattle industry in the 1860s. **(8 marks)**

> Cattle trails were very important to the cattle industry.
> Cowboys herded large herds of cattle from Texas to the railheads in Kansas and Missouri.
> Animals worth $5 in Texas could be sold for $40 in Chicago.
> Cattle were loaded onto trains at railheads.
> The trails helped make some people very rich.

- **a.** Experiment with different ways of linking some or all of the points using the techniques you have learned.

- **b.** Look carefully at all of the sentences you have written. Which ones work well, clearly and briefly linking ideas? Which do not? Explain your thinking.

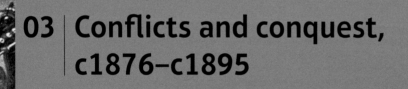

03 | Conflicts and conquest, c1876–c1895

In 1876, a bad defeat for the US Army by the Plains Indians changed government attitudes. But by 1877, resistance from the Plains Indians was all but over.

Farming on the Plains had made great progress due to new technology and improvements in farming methods. This put more pressure on the government to give more Indian reservation land to white American homesteaders.

The good years for the cattle industry on the Plains came to an end in the terrible winter of 1886–87. This meant changes for the lives of cowboys, and worsened conflicts between big ranchers and homesteaders. It caused more problems for law and order, with range wars involving gunslingers like Billy the Kid and Wyatt Earp.

For the Plains Indians, after 1876 reservations were cut down to small bits of territory and different methods were used to destroy Plains Indian culture, so Plains Indians would stop resisting the spread of 'civilisation' and accept the American way of life.

Learning outcomes

By the end of this chapter, you will:

- understand how changes in farming, the cattle industry and settlement affected the West
- understand the ways in which conflict and tension in the West increased because of different ideas about how the land should be used
- understand how government policies for dealing with the Plains Indians led to the destruction of their way of life.

3.1 Changes in farming, the cattle industry and settlement

Changes in farming

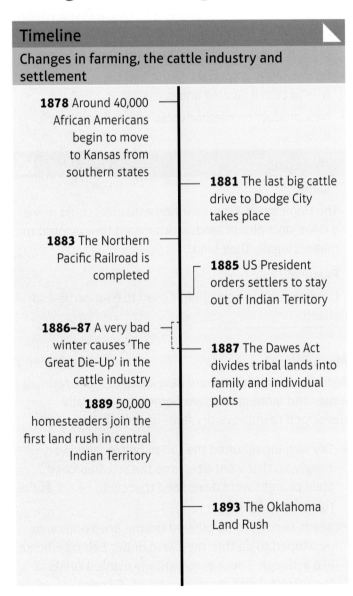

Timeline

Changes in farming, the cattle industry and settlement

1878 Around 40,000 African Americans begin to move to Kansas from southern states

1881 The last big cattle drive to Dodge City takes place

1883 The Northern Pacific Railroad is completed

1885 US President orders settlers to stay out of Indian Territory

1886–87 A very bad winter causes 'The Great Die-Up' in the cattle industry

1887 The Dawes Act divides tribal lands into family and individual plots

1889 50,000 homesteaders join the first land rush in central Indian Territory

1893 The Oklahoma Land Rush

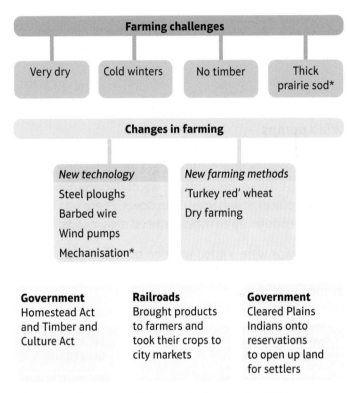

Farming challenges

| Very dry | Cold winters | No timber | Thick prairie sod* |

Changes in farming

New technology
Steel ploughs
Barbed wire
Wind pumps
Mechanisation*

New farming methods
'Turkey red' wheat
Dry farming

Government
Homestead Act and Timber and Culture Act

Railroads
Brought products to farmers and took their crops to city markets

Government
Cleared Plains Indians onto reservations to open up land for settlers

Figure 3.1 Summary of changes in farming by 1876.

In the period 1876–95, the new technologies and methods shown in Figure 3.1 began to have an impact. As a result, by the 1890s, homestead farming was beginning to turn the Plains into very good farmland.

Key terms

Prairie sod*

The tough grass on the Plains with dense roots made the top layer of the ground – the sod – difficult to break up.

Mechanisation*

Using machines to do work rather than people or animals.

The impact of new farming methods

The government paid for scientific experiments to develop new methods to help farming in the West.

Dry farming

Dry farming aimed to keep water in the soil. One method was developed by Hardy Webster Campbell, who started homesteading in the Dakota Territory in 1879. Dry farming prepared the soil so that it trapped rainwater under the surface. Campbell's techniques also meant the crops grew stronger roots, which meant they could get more water from the soil. Farmers found that dry farming worked well with wheat. Agricultural experts promoted dry farming methods as the best way for homesteaders to farm the Plains, but it was not used widely until the 1900s.

The impact of new technology

Wind pumps

Many farmers in the 1860s and 1870s gave up on their claims* because they could not get enough water for their crops. There was plenty of water underground but, in many places, it was very deep down. There was no way to bring enough up to meet farmers' daily needs.

Wind pumps were a good solution but there were serious problems with using them on the Great Plains, as the figure shows.

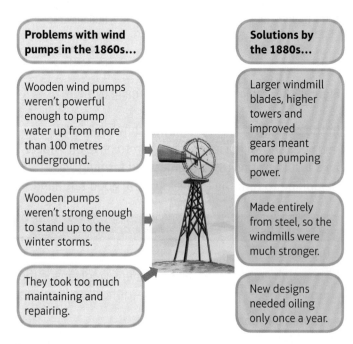

Problems with wind pumps in the 1860s...

Wooden wind pumps weren't powerful enough to pump water up from more than 100 metres underground.

Wooden pumps weren't strong enough to stand up to the winter storms.

They took too much maintaining and repairing.

Solutions by the 1880s...

Larger windmill blades, higher towers and improved gears meant more pumping power.

Made entirely from steel, so the windmills were much stronger.

New designs needed oiling only once a year.

Figure: Improvements in wind pumps from the 1860s to the 1880s.

As a result of the improvements made by the 1880s, windpumps were used all over the West by both cattle ranchers and farmers. The biggest problem facing farmers in the West had been mostly solved.

Barbed wire

First introduced in 1874, barbed wire had a huge impact on farming in the West.

- With timber being hard to find, barbed wire was a cheap way for farmers to fence off their claims and protect their crops from roaming livestock.
- In the 1880s, cattle ranchers also began to use barbed wire to keep their cows on their ranch and to stop other people's animals getting onto their pasture*.
- By the 1880s, a special coating had been added to the wire to stop it rusting and breaking.
- New production methods also reduced how much it cost.

> ### Key terms
>
> #### Claims*
> The Homestead Act meant homesteaders could make a claim on a plot of land, which meant they wanted to make it legally their land.
>
> #### Pasture*
> Land covered in grass that is used to feed cattle and sheep.

Mechanisation

Agricultural machines were developed to make farming easier and more productive. Some were specially developed to improve dry farming techniques.

- Dry farming required the soil to be ploughed very deeply, so that went deep into the soil. Improved steel ploughs were developed that could be set at the right depth for this.
- Seeds needed to be planted deeply. Seed drills were developed to do this: they were drawn behind a horse, like a plough. These automatically planted seeds at the correct depth for successful dry farming.

Mechanisation made farming faster, more efficient and more productive. Successful homesteaders could farm larger areas using the new machines.

Source A

This poster from 1876 was part of a promotional campaign to publicise the benefits of barbed wire to farmers and railroad companies.

Activities

1 Explain why the wind pump was important in the development of farming in the West. Use information from previous chapters to give a full answer.

2 Complete this paragraph starter: 'The railroads helped the development of farming in the West by....'

Key term

Overstocked*

The situation when too many animals are relying on the same area of pasture: the grass gets eaten up, the soil is damaged and animals can become weak as a result of hunger.

Drought*

When there are severe shortages of water because it hasn't rained for a long time.

Changes in the cattle industry

Through the 1870s, so much money went into cattle ranching that the open range became overstocked*. This had several serious consequences for the cattle industry in the 1880s.

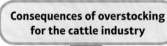
Consequences of overstocking for the cattle industry

Lower prices
- So many cows were being sold that the price of beef fell.
- Profits from cattle ranching also fell.
- Ranchers kept their cattle instead of selling them, hoping that prices would rise.

Damage to pasture land
- So many cattle were on the open range that they damaged the soil.
- There was a drought* in 1883 that killed a lot of grass.
- Without enough grass to eat, many cows became weak.

The 'Great Die-Up'
- The winter of 1886–87 was very bad. Temperatures dropped as low as –55°C.
- At least 15% of cattle on the open range died.
- Many cattlemen had to leave the cattle industry.

Figure: Problems in the cattle industry in the 1880s.

Cattle that survived into the spring of 1887 were often in very poor condition, but everyone tried to sell what they had, making beef prices fall even lower. Together, these factors put an end to ranching on the open range.

Large ranches found it difficult to look after cattle during the winter because they were spread over a large area. Smaller ranches coped better, though many had to take out large bank loans to survive. After 1887, ranches were smaller.

There were many benefits of having a smaller ranch.

- Smaller herds could **easily be found** when the snows came, and provided with shelter and food.
- In times of drought, it was **easier to provide water** to the herd using wind pumps.
- Smaller herds were **easier to guard**, so cattlemen could start to get more control over rustling*.
- Smaller herds **reduced the supply of beef**, so meat could be sold for higher prices.
- After 1887, ranchers moved to producing **high-quality meat**. Ranchers began fencing in their land with barbed wire to keep their cattle separate from other lower quality breeds.

Key term

Rustling*

Stealing livestock.

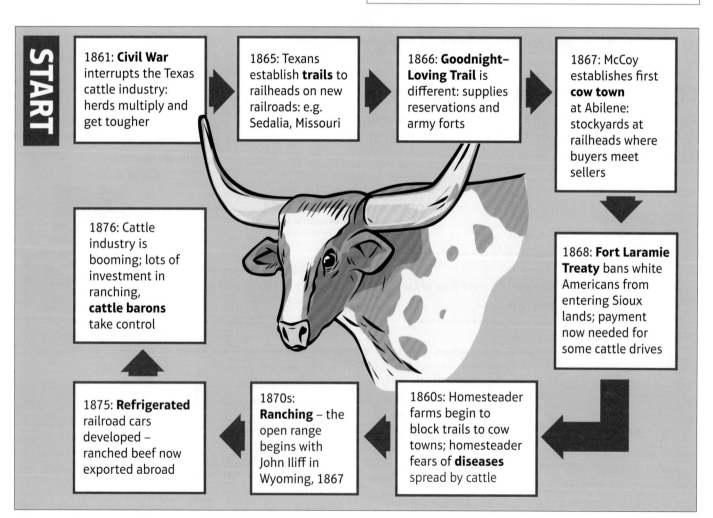

Figure 3.2 Summary of changes in the cattle industry by 1876.

START

1861: **Civil War** interrupts the Texas cattle industry: herds multiply and get tougher

1865: Texans establish **trails** to railheads on new railroads: e.g. Sedalia, Missouri

1866: **Goodnight–Loving Trail** is different: supplies reservations and army forts

1867: McCoy establishes first **cow town** at Abilene: stockyards at railheads where buyers meet sellers

1868: **Fort Laramie Treaty** bans white Americans from entering Sioux lands; payment now needed for some cattle drives

1860s: Homesteader farms begin to block trails to cow towns; homesteader fears of **diseases** spread by cattle

1870s: **Ranching** – the open range begins with John Iliff in Wyoming, 1867

1875: **Refrigerated** railroad cars developed – ranched beef now exported abroad

1876: Cattle industry is booming; lots of investment in ranching, **cattle barons** take control

As some ranchers went out of business, the homesteaders moved in. In some parts of the Great Plains the open range disappeared. It was either fenced off as ranches or ploughed up for farms.

The impact of the end of the open range

The terrible winter of 1886–87 was called the 'Great Die-Up' because of the huge losses in the herds of the open range. The end of the open range meant that fewer cowboys were needed. Those that remained in the cattle industry got jobs as ranch hands.

- The life of a ranch hand was not adventurous. Ranch hands did jobs around the ranch, such as branding* cattle, looking after horses and calves and mending fences.
- They lived in bunkhouses, which were often not very comfortable – leaking roofs, thin walls and beds full of lice. There were rules to follow.
- They were responsible for 'riding the line': patrolling the boundary between one ranch and another.

Key term

Branding*
A mark burnt into skin using a heated piece of metal.

Activity ?

Copy the graph below to show how the life of Texas cowboys changed between 1860 and 1890. Draw a line on the graph showing how the cowboys' level of freedom changed. Think about what events marked turning points in their work.

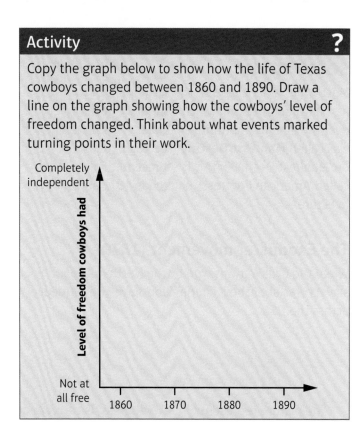

Exam-style question, Section A ○

Explain **two** consequences of the winter of 1886–87 for the cattle industry. **8 marks**

Exam tip ○

Remember that the question is not asking you to describe the events of the winter of 1886–87, or the causes of the 'Great Die-Up'. Instead, it wants an explanation of two developments that happened to the cattle industry *as a result of* this winter.

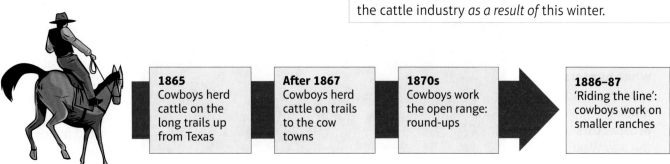

1865
Cowboys herd cattle on the long trails up from Texas

After 1867
Cowboys herd cattle on trails to the cow towns

1870s
Cowboys work the open range: round-ups

1886–87
'Riding the line': cowboys work on smaller ranches

Figure 3.3 Changes in cowboy work from the end of the Civil War to after the winter of 1886–87.

The continued growth of settlement

Most white Americans saw the settlement of the West as a natural process in which a superior* race took over the land from primitive peoples . This process was called **Manifest Destiny** (see page 20 for more on 'Manifest Destiny'). This is represented in a picture called 'American Progress', painted in 1872 and shown in Figure 3.4.

The Exoduster movement (1879)

When the Civil War was won by the North in 1865, slavery was abolished. Four million slaves were freed across the USA.

However, many white people in the southern states could not accept that black Americans should be free. Southern whites did everything they could to keep black Americans from becoming independent.

- They used violence and fear to stop black Americans voting.
- They also refused to sell land to black Americans and forced them into sharecropping*, which kept black farmers working for free on white plantation farms.

Key terms

Superior*

Better, more advanced.

Sharecropping*

When a landowner allows a tenant to use some of their land in return for a share of the crops they grow.

The picture represents **Manifest Destiny**. White Americans believed they had a mission from God to settle in America.

'Progress' is carrying a school textbook, representing education, and is unwinding **telegraph wires**. These are symbols of progress and civilisation.

The American Indians have only unsaddled horses and a travois. The settlers have wagons pulled by oxen, there is a stagecoach and then three lines of **railroads**.

The East is the centre of civilisation from which progress is spreading out to the West.

American Indians are shown running away from Progress. Buffalo and other wild animals are fleeing, too.

White **hunters, explorers** and **mining prospectors** lead the way West.

White **settlers** are shown making the land useful and productive: ploughing it for crops, fencing it in and building houses.

Development of white settlement

Figure 3.4 'American Progress', painted by John Gast in 1872. Other titles for the painting are 'Westward the course of destiny' and 'Manifest destiny'. The giant floating woman represents 'Progress'.

The 'Exodus'

Because the oppression* of black Americans continued in the South after the Civil War, some black Americans decided to move to the West and set up homesteads. A former slave called **Benjamin Singleton** set up a settlement in Kansas in 1873. Singleton promoted Kansas as a place for black Americans to live. He held meetings and placed newspaper adverts in the southern states, showing Kansas as a good place to live. He helped many hundreds of black Americans to move to Kansas.

In 1879, a rumour spread that the federal government had given the whole state of Kansas to ex-slaves for them to settle. This was not true, but by the end of 1879, 40,000 black Americans had set off west, heading for Kansas and also Missouri, Indiana and Illinois. The black settlers were called the **Exodusters** because they moved in great numbers, and reminded people of the Jews escaping from Egypt in a part of the Bible called 'Exodus'.

Source B

'En route to Kansas': a picture from 1879, based on a sketch by H. J. Lewis that was published in *Harper's Weekly* magazine. It shows a family of Exodusters on their way to Kansas.

Singleton and the rumour about free land in Kansas were not the only reasons for the Exodusters.

- Many black Americans had started moving within the southern states since the Civil War, looking for better jobs and opportunities.
- Kansas had been well-known as an anti-slavery state, so black Americans thought they would be welcome there.
- The Homestead Act offered the promise of free land: a major 'pull' factor* for the migrants.
- The Bible story of the Exodus also provided a religious 'push' factor*: some migrants prayed that God would help them escape oppression.

Key terms

Oppression*

Treating a group of people unfairly or cruelly and stopping them from having the same rights as others.

'Pull' factor*

Something that attracts ('pulls') migrants towards a country, city, etc.

'Push' factor*

Something that 'pushes' migrants away from their original homes, for example, low wages.

👤 Oppression in the southern states

👤 Religious beliefs about escaping slavery and oppression

👤 Benjamin Singleton's campaign

👤 Rumours about free land in Kansas

👤 Kansas' reputation as a state that had fought to end slavery

👤 The Homestead Act

Figure: Push and pull factors: Reasons for the Exoduster movement, 1879.

Impacts of the Exoduster movement

- **Impacts for settlement of the West:** by 1880, there were 43,107 black Americans in Kansas. New settlements were founded.

- **Impacts for the black American settlers:** other settlers had already taken all the best land in Kansas. The Exodusters were left with land which was very difficult to farm. Many had come to Kansas without enough money to live on, and they soon needed help.

- **Response from the Kansas government:** many Exodusters had travelled through areas affected by yellow fever and so many were very ill. The Kansas governor found them places to live and organised some money to help them get started.

- **Responses from white Americans:** there was huge opposition to the Exodusters in the southern states. Most white Americans in Kansas also thought it was wrong that the state government should help the Exodusters and not them.

- **End of the movement:** problems faced by the Exodusters in Kansas became known in the South, so by the 1880s, a lot fewer migrants made the trip. Those who did had usually saved up money and were better prepared for settling in the West. Even so, Exoduster migrants typically remained poorer than the white migrants to Kansas through the 1880s and 1890s, though they were better off than they had been in the South.

> ### Activity **?**
>
> How different was the Exoduster movement from the Mormon migration and settlement of the Great Salt Lake region (see page 22)? Identify as many similarities and differences as you can.
>
> For example:
>
> - Similarities: both the black Americans and the Mormons were being treated badly by other Americans (push factor).
> - Differences: the Mormons did not expect any help in settling the Great Salt Lake region and so planned their migration very carefully.

The Oklahoma Land Rush (1893)

Indian Territory was land set up for American Indian settlement by the Indian Removal Act of 1830 (page 16).

Indian Territory was divided up into different sections for different tribes. In the middle of the Territory, there was a section that was not officially given to one particular tribe. White settlers had been trying to move into this middle section since the start of the 1880s, but the US Army moved them off again as Indian Territory was not open to white settlement.

Then, in 1889, the US government decided to open up the middle section of Indian Territory for white American settlement. The land was divided up into 160-acre sections. It was announced that at 12 noon on 22 April 1889, the area would be opened for claims. Thousands of hopeful settlers waited on the boundary of the unopened territory and then, once a signal was given, everyone rushed over the boundary to reach a section and claim it as theirs. This process was called a land rush.

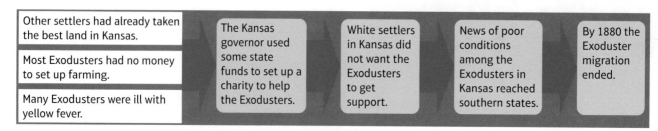

Figure: Reasons for the end of the Exoduster migration.

Source C

Oklahoma Run painted by Robert Lindneux in 1889.

There were seven land rushes in Oklahoma, starting with the land rush of 1889, with the last happening in 1895. The largest land rush was in 1893, when eight million acres of Indian Territory was opened up for settlement.

Although the US government had always claimed to be protecting Plains Indian land from white Americans, this protection never lasted long. The government gave in to pressure from white settlers who wanted the Plains Indians' land, and found ways to move the Plains Indians somewhere else, until there was nowhere left for them to live as free Plains Indians at all.

Exam-style question, Section A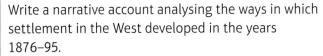

Write a narrative account analysing the ways in which settlement in the West developed in the years 1876–95.

You may use the following in your answer:

- The Exoduster movement (1879)
- The Oklahoma Land Rush (1893).

You **must** also use information of your own.   **8 marks**

Exam tip

Avoid just telling the story of, for example, the Exodusters. Instead, link what you know about changes in settlement.

Activity   ?

Study Source C. Explain what made these people so hungry for land.

Summary

- Changes in farming solved most of the early problems the homesteaders had faced.
- The end of the 'open range' meant new, smaller ranches, fenced with barbed wire.
- The Exoduster movement brought black American settlers to the Plains, while the Oklahoma Land Rush opened up land to settlers from previously protected Indian Territory.

Checkpoint

Strengthen

S1 Explain which farming problem of the West was solved by wind pumps.

S2 Explain the consequences of the winter of 1886–87 for the cattle industry.

Challenge

C1 How successful were white settlers and ranchers at living on the Plains? Were they more or less successful than the Plains Indians? What factors helped them? What factors set them back? Explain your answer.

How confident do you feel about your answers? Try linking up developments across all three chapters of this book – e.g. farming problems (1), tackling the problems (2) and solving the problems (3).

3.2 Conflict and tension

Learning outcomes

- Understand ways in which crime, conflict and lawlessness continued to grow in the West and how government and local communities responded to this.
- Understand how the Johnson County War of 1892 came about and its consequences.
- Understand the reasons for the Battle of the Little Big Horn, and its consequences through to the Wounded Knee Massacre of 1890.

Continued problems of law and order

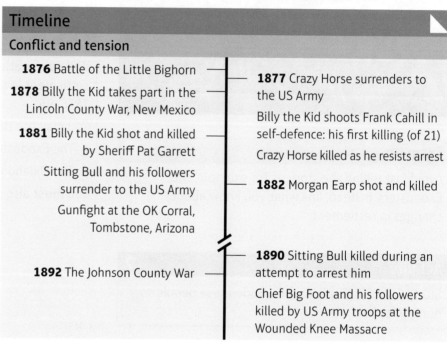

Timeline

Conflict and tension

1876 Battle of the Little Bighorn

1877 Crazy Horse surrenders to the US Army

Billy the Kid shoots Frank Cahill in self-defence: his first killing (of 21)

1878 Billy the Kid takes part in the Lincoln County War, New Mexico

1881 Billy the Kid shot and killed by Sheriff Pat Garrett

Sitting Bull and his followers surrender to the US Army

Gunfight at the OK Corral, Tombstone, Arizona

Crazy Horse killed as he resists arrest

1882 Morgan Earp shot and killed

1890 Sitting Bull killed during an attempt to arrest him

Chief Big Foot and his followers killed by US Army troops at the Wounded Knee Massacre

1892 The Johnson County War

The development of the West often led to conflicts and tensions between people as they struggled to make a living.

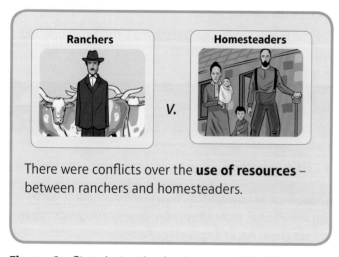

There were conflicts over the **use of resources** – between ranchers and homesteaders.

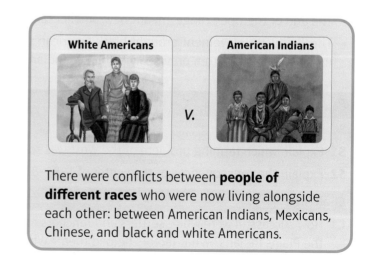

There were conflicts between **people of different races** who were now living alongside each other: between American Indians, Mexicans, Chinese, and black and white Americans.

Figure: Conflicts during the development of the West.

Poverty
Most people struggled to make a living. Stealing was hard to resist.

Conflict over resources
There was conflict over resources such as land and water between ranchers and homesteaders, big ranchers and small ranchers, settlers and Plains Indians.

Fear and intimidation
People were afraid to act against powerful gangs: whether they were gangs of criminals or of powerful businessmen.

Independent attitudes
Men were expected to sort out their own problems, using violence if necessary. Killing in self-defence was accepted by law.

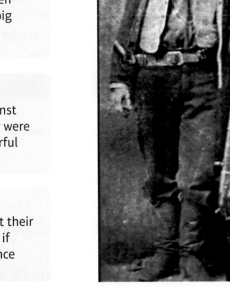

Geography
Territories in the West were large areas with lots of places for gangs to hide from justice.

Weak justice system
Governors and law officers were often corrupt – local gangs paid them money so they weren't arrested.

Problematic lawmen
There was a shortage of reliable men to be lawmen. Lawmen were often former outlaws themselves.

Vigilantes
Criminals who had been arrested were sometimes taken away from lawmen and lynched (hanged). People did not have much respect for the law.

Figure 3.5 Billy the Kid and lawlessness in the West.

Billy the Kid (1859–81)

- **Early life:** Billy the Kid grew up in mining camps in New Mexico. He never held down a steady job and, when he was 14 or 15, he got into trouble for stealing butter. Billy later stole horses and rustled cattle. Billy became notorious for being able to escape from jails.

- **Lincoln County War:** in 1878, Billy became involved in a conflict over resources between cattle baron John Chisum, who had a huge ranch in New Mexico, and settlers and other ranchers desperate for land. Billy fought on Chisum's side against the settlers.

- **Billy's private war:** although the Lincoln County War soon ended, Billy swore to kill everyone responsible for the death of a friend in the war. He and his gang had many hideouts around the county and a lot of support from local people.

- **Law and order:** local ranchers appealed to the president to end the violence in New Mexico. A new sheriff was also elected, with the job of bringing Billy to justice. The sheriff's name was Pat Garrett.

- **Billy's capture, escape and death:** Garrett tracked Billy down, captured him and brought him to court. He was sentenced to death, but the guards at the jail were careless and Billy made a dramatic escape. Garrett tracked him again to Fort Sumner and shot him dead.

Activity ?

Study Figure 3.5 which shows the main factors leading to lawlessness in the West. Now read the information about Billy the Kid. Which of the factors about lawlessness could you link to the life of Billy the Kid?

Although Billy the Kid was a thief and a murderer, he was seen as an exciting, reckless, romantic figure by many. He was significant in the problems of law and order for three main reasons:

1 **Powerless people** (the poor, ethnic minorities, small homesteaders and ranchers) liked the way he stood up against the big northern businessmen.

2 Most of his involvement in violence was as a **hired gun** in a war between cattle barons* and those who dared challenge their control of the land.

3 The **justice system** in Lincoln County was too weak and corrupt to deal with Billy and his gang. Garrett said after Billy escaped from jail: 'I knew now that I would have to kill the Kid.'

Wyatt Earp and the OK Corral* (1881)

In the cow towns, cowboys often spent their money on drinking, dancing, gambling and prostitutes. Businessmen also came to the cow towns to make money. They were not prepared to put up with wild, drunken cowboys. These businessmen wanted sheriffs and marshals in their towns to keep order. They chose men like Wyatt Earp (1848–1929) to be sheriffs and marshals – tough men who would force troublemakers to behave or leave town.

Key terms

Cattle barons*

Very rich businessmen who controlled the cattle industry.

Corral*

An enclosure for cattle or horses.

Boom town*

A town that grows out of nothing very quickly.

Wyatt Earp: key events

Wyatt Earp becomes a lawman after helping to stop cowboys who were making trouble in Wichita	In May 1874, Wyatt Earp was involved in a fight in the cow town of Wichita and was arrested. Just then, a rowdy group of cowboys started making trouble in the town. Earp helped the deputy marshal to restore order. As a result, the mayor of Wichita offered him the job of deputy marshal. After a time as marshal in Dodge City, Earp moved to Tombstone, Arizona Territory in 1879.
Tombstone's conflict was between rich businessmen and ranchers	Tombstone was a boom town* and was controlled by rich businessmen. There was conflict between the businessmen and a gang of ranchers led by the Clanton and the McLaury families. In 1880, the rich businessmen hired Wyatt Earp as deputy sheriff to bring order to the town.
Tombstone becomes increasingly lawless	There were clashes between the Earps (Wyatt and his two brothers), and the ranchers, as the lawmen tried to recover stolen horses. In 1881, the cowboys rustled cattle and robbed stagecoaches. Rumours spread that the Earps had been involved in the stagecoach robberies but the Earps said this wasn't true.
The Earps win the gunfight at the OK Corral	In a gunfight on 26 October 1881, near Tombstone's OK Corral, the Earps killed Tom and Frank McLaury and Billy Clanton. The Earps said that they had intended only to disarm the men, but they opened fire first. Some townspeople doubted this story.
The Earps and cowboys continue to fight each other 	Trouble continued. Cowboys shot and killed one of Wyatt's brothers in 1882. Wyatt shot the two men he claimed were responsible. Opinion turned against the Earps because their violent approach to law-keeping had only caused more conflict. Wyatt had become a murderer with no regard for the law. Wyatt was forced to flee Tombstone.

Not every town was like Tombstone. In general, lawlessness **decreased** as settlements developed. People needed their businesses and their families to be safe. So residents voted for town governments that passed laws to ban guns within their town. As a result, most towns in the West were peaceful.

The railroads and electric telegraph also reduced lawlessness.

- Law officers and judges could keep in close touch with their bosses in state government and ask for support when they needed it.

- In turn, state government could make sure local law officers were doing their job. Corruption was harder to get away with.

- Federal government had closer links with their marshals. People would no longer put up with corrupt lawmen who broke the law, like the Earps.

Key term

Jury*

A group of twelve ordinary people who listen to the details of a court case and decide whether someone is guilty or not.

The range wars, including the Johnson County War

The armed conflicts over control of land were known as 'range wars'. Range wars' were named after the wide open Plains land that cattle roamed across. The best-known of all the range wars was the Johnson County War.

The Johnson County War was a range war between cattle barons on one side, and homesteaders and small ranchers on the other. Even by the 1890s, the West still had places where men took the law into their own hands.

The Johnson County War (1892)

Tensions in Wyoming

In 1870, there were only 9,000 US citizens in the whole of Wyoming Territory and almost all the land was owned by the government. Through the 1870s, huge cattle ranches developed. But the winter of 1886–87 (the 'Great Die-Up') caused terrible losses to their herds. The big ranchers were no longer so powerful.

Small ranchers survived the winter of 1886-87 a bit better than the big ranches. The big ranchers believed this was because the small ranchers had stolen many of their cows. Rustling had been a problem for many years on the open range. The big ranchers were in charge of organising the spring round-up. They banned the small ranchers from the spring round-up.

Ordinary people – homesteaders and small ranchers – were tired of the way the big ranchers always grabbed everything for themselves. Juries* made up of ordinary people would almost never convict someone accused of rustling by the big ranchers in Johnson County. Big ranchers began to discuss taking the law into their own hands.

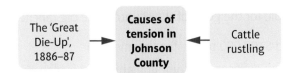

Figure: What caused tension in Johnson Country?

The killing of Ella Watson and Jim Averill

The Johnson County War began after a series of murders in the county.

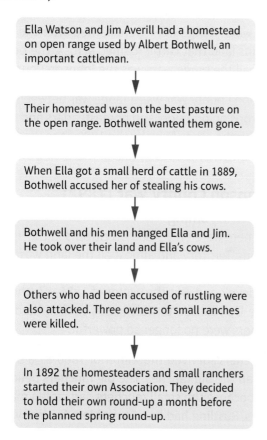

Ella Watson and Jim Averill had a homestead on open range used by Albert Bothwell, an important cattleman.

↓

Their homestead was on the best pasture on the open range. Bothwell wanted them gone.

↓

When Ella got a small herd of cattle in 1889, Bothwell accused her of stealing his cows.

↓

Bothwell and his men hanged Ella and Jim. He took over their land and Ella's cows.

↓

Others who had been accused of rustling were also attacked. Three owners of small ranches were killed.

↓

In 1892 the homesteaders and small ranchers started their own Association. They decided to hold their own round-up a month before the planned spring round-up.

Figure: Why Ella Watson and Jim Averill were killed.

The plan for an early round-up was a threat to the big ranch owners. The homesteaders and small ranchers would be able to claim all the unbranded spring calves for themselves.

The invasion of Johnson County

The big ranchers had had enough. They planned a full-scale invasion of Johnson County, to kill 70 men who 'should die for the good of the country'. The big ranchers:

- raised $100,000 to pay for the invasion
- told the governor of Wyoming about their plan
- hired 22 gunmen from Texas
- promised the gunmen a $50 bonus for every rustler from the list that they killed.

However, the Texan gunmen known as the 'Invaders' failed in their mission. Learning that two men from their hit list, Nate Champion and Nick Ray, were at a ranch called the KC Ranch, they abandoned their original plan and attacked the ranch instead. Nate held them off all day from the ranch's sturdy log cabin but was eventually shot and killed.

Sheriff Angus of Johnson County heard about the attack. He was on the side of the homesteaders and small ranchers. He quickly raised a force of 40 men and went after the Invaders. Outraged citizens of Buffalo, Johnson County's main town, also joined the resistance against the Invaders because they were sick of the big ranchers acting as if they owned everything and everyone. The Invaders defended themselves at a ranch called the TA Ranch, surrounded by 300 angry Johnson County residents. Three days later, the US 6th Cavalry arrived and ended the siege.

Source A

This photo of the Invaders was taken during their arrest, in spring 1892, when they were held (in comfortable conditions) at an army fort outside Johnson County.

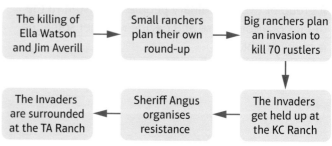

The killing of Ella Watson and Jim Averill → Small ranchers plan their own round-up → Big ranchers plan an invasion to kill 70 rustlers ↓ The Invaders are surrounded at the TA Ranch ← Sheriff Angus organises resistance ← The Invaders get held up at the KC Ranch

Figure: The invasion of Johnson County.

The trial

The Invaders had powerful friends: the state governor, the judge, the Wyoming US marshal and two US senators supported the big ranchers and its violent plan to end rustling in Johnson County.

- The governor made sure the Invaders were taken out of Johnson County to be held in Fort Fetterman, in case citizens tried to lynch them.
- The best Chicago lawyers were hired by the big ranchers to defend the Invaders.
- The lawyers convinced the judge to move the trial to Cheyenne, the state capital. Jury members here were more likely to favour rich, respectable men over a bunch of rustlers.
- Knowing that Johnson County was short of money, the lawyers delayed the trial as much as they could until the prosecutors had run out of money. Once the prosecution could no longer afford the trial costs, the charges against the accused had to be dropped.

Source B

An unknown local newspaper expressed its outrage at the actions of respectable, important men and state officials.

```
[They] banded together in a murderous
attempt to override and trample under foot
every [trace] of law and order... If a man
murders, punish him according to law for his
crime whether he be a 'rustler', a cattleman
or a state official.
```

Significance of the Johnson County War

Through the 19th century, people in the West had used vigilante justice*. What is important about the Johnson County War is that on this occasion, so many people stood up to the big ranchers' plan to kill 70 people and acted to prevent vigilante justice.

Key term

Vigilante justice*

When a group decides to punish criminals themselves because they do not trust the law to do it.

Reducing tensions

After the winter of 1886–87, most cattlemen moved to small ranches with fenced-in winter pastures. This reduced tensions between farms and ranches because now it was clear who owned what.

Activity ?

Supply endings for each of these three sentences:

a One consequence of the Johnson County War was…

b The Johnson County War was important for law and order because…

c The Johnson County War was important for homesteaders because…

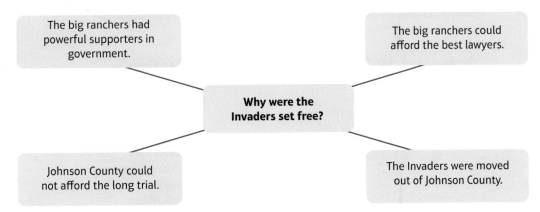

Figure: Why the Invaders were set free.

Conflict with the Plains Indians

From the 1830s to the 1870s, Plains Indian tribes had agreed treaties with the US government, only to see those treaties fail each time. Figure 3.6 summarises key events in this process up to the end of Red Cloud's War.

The Battle of the Little Big Horn

The Battle of the Little Big Horn in 1876 was a turning point in the history of the American West. In this battle, the US Army was defeated by the Sioux nation. The shock of this defeat changed the US policy towards the Plains Indians. From then on, the policy was that Plains Indians had to assimilate* or die.

Key term
Assimilate*
To become like something else: for the Plains Indians, it meant becoming US citizens and rejecting all their old culture, beliefs and ways of life.

Conflict over the Black Hills

In 1874, the Northern Pacific Railroad was approaching Sioux hunting grounds in Dakota. US Army commander George Custer led an expedition of the 7th Cavalry to protect the railroad builders from Plains Indian attacks. However, Custer also used his mission to prospect for gold in the Black Hills. Within six months, thousands of prospectors followed. This broke the 1868 Fort Laramie Treaty.

- The US government offered to buy the Black Hills from the Sioux for $6 million. The Sioux refused. Attacks by the Sioux continued on prospectors. The government said this meant the Sioux had broken the Fort Laramie Treaty.

- Believing that the US government had betrayed them, thousands of Sioux and Cheyenne warriors left their reservations to join Sioux leaders: Sitting Bull and Crazy Horse.

- In December 1875, the government ordered the Sioux to return to their reservations. They were given 60 days to obey. After this, President Grant stated, any Sioux outside the reservations could be attacked.

- Deep snows made it impossible for all the Sioux to obey President Grant's order, even if they had wanted to. By the spring of 1876, more than 7,000 Sioux, including 2,000 warriors, had gathered together. Chief Sitting Bull said: 'The whites want a war and we will give it to them.'

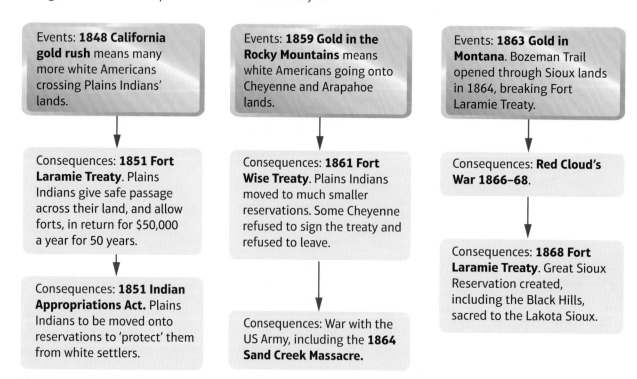

Events: **1848 California gold rush** means many more white Americans crossing Plains Indians' lands.

↓

Consequences: **1851 Fort Laramie Treaty**. Plains Indians give safe passage across their land, and allow forts, in return for $50,000 a year for 50 years.

↓

Consequences: **1851 Indian Appropriations Act**. Plains Indians to be moved onto reservations to 'protect' them from white settlers.

Events: **1859 Gold in the Rocky Mountains** means white Americans going onto Cheyenne and Arapahoe lands.

↓

Consequences: **1861 Fort Wise Treaty**. Plains Indians moved to much smaller reservations. Some Cheyenne refused to sign the treaty and refused to leave.

↓

Consequences: War with the US Army, including the **1864 Sand Creek Massacre.**

Events: **1863 Gold in Montana**. Bozeman Trail opened through Sioux lands in 1864, breaking Fort Laramie Treaty.

↓

Consequences: **Red Cloud's War 1866–68**.

↓

Consequences: **1868 Fort Laramie Treaty**. Great Sioux Reservation created, including the Black Hills, sacred to the Lakota Sioux.

Figure 3.6 Key events and their consequences in the conflicts over use of the Plains Indians' lands 1848–68.

Battle of the Little Bighorn (June 1876)

The US Army planned to attack the Sioux to force them back to their reservations. Custer's scouts found a camp of 2,000 warriors in the valley of the Little Bighorn.

Custer did not wait for reinforcements, and led 200 of his men into the Little Bighorn valley. Sitting Bull got the women and children of the tribes to safety while Crazy Horse led an attack. Greatly outnumbered, Custer and all his 200 men were killed.

- **Plains Indians must be kept on their reservations.** The US Army would not stop going after the Sioux and Cheyenne tribes. Within five years, almost all the Sioux and Cheyenne were confined to reservations, completely dependent on the US government for food and shelter.
- **Previous treaties could be ignored.** The government decided that some Plains Indians no longer had any rights to their old treaty deals. Plains Indians were moved onto smaller reservations in worse conditions than before. The Sioux were told that if they did not give up the Black Hills, the US government would stop sending them food. Faced with starvation, the Sioux gave up the Black Hills.
- **Military control of Plains Indians must be maintained.** The Sioux's weapons and horses were taken and they had to live under military rule. The number of soldiers and forts in the region increased.

Plains Indian resistance to the loss of their land was effectively over.

Impacts of the battle

Little Big Horn changed how white Americans saw the Plains Indians. Instead of seeing them as weak savages, white Americans now felt threatened.

There was enormous pressure on the US government to crush the Plains Indians' resistance. This had catastrophic consequences on Plains Indians and their way of life.

Source C

This depiction of the Battle of the Little Bighorn is by White Bird, a Cheyenne Indian who was present at the battle. White Bird created the picture in 1894 or 1895.

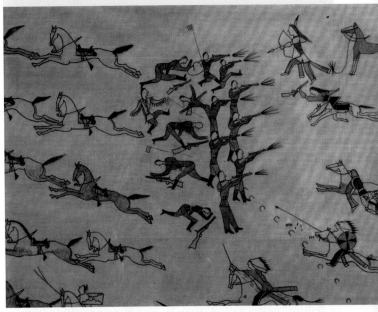

Source D

From and article in the *Chicago Tribune*, 7 July 1876.

It is time to quit this Sunday School policy, and let Sheridan [the Commander-in-Chief of the army in the West]... exterminate every Indian who will not remain upon the reservations. The best use to make of an Indian who will not stay on a reservation is to kill him. It is time that the dawdling [slow and aimless], maudlin [foolishly sentimental] peace-policy was abandoned.

Exam-style question, Section A

Explain **two** consequences of the Battle of the Little Bighorn (1876).   **8 marks**

Exam tip

First identify two things that happened as a result of the Battle of the Little Bighorn – for example, Plains Indians being forced to give up their weapons.

Then explain why this happened as a result of the Battle of the Little Bighorn – for example, the government wanted to make sure the Plains Indians could never attack US troops again.

The Wounded Knee Massacre (1890)

By the end of the 1880s, the situation on the reservations was bad. The government had cut rations to some Sioux reservations just as a drought hit, in 1890. The drought meant Sioux crops died.

The Ghost Dance

A Paiute Indian called Wovoka had a vision telling him that if Plains Indians rejected white ways of life and danced a sacred dance, the Great Spirit would carry away the white people in a great flood and the land would belong to the Plains Indians again.

The Ghost Dance spread rapidly through the reservations. US President Harrison ordered the army into the reservations to take control. Sitting Bull was killed in an attempt to arrest him. The army believed Sitting Bull was planning to lead the Ghost Dancers in a rebellion. This was not true.

The Wounded Knee Massacre (29 December 1890)

Sitting Bull's followers fled south and joined the band of Big Foot, another refugee from a reservation. The army caught up with them and took them to Wounded Knee Creek. A Sioux warrior resisted being disarmed and others began to dance.

In the general confusion, a shot was fired. The 7th Cavalry opened fire. In ten minutes, 250 Sioux were dead. Half the dead were women and children.

Source E

This photo from January 1891 shows US Army soldiers burying the dead after the Wounded Knee Massacre.

Reactions to the Wounded Knee Massacre

Public opinion of the Massacre was generally positive in the USA. Soldiers who took part in the Massacre were praised and the public was relieved that the Ghost Dance was over.

- This reaction suggests that most white Americans thought Plains Indians needed to be killed if they could not be controlled on reservations.

- Public opinion and the US Army also saw Wounded Knee as revenge for the Battle of the Little Bighorn.

- In 1890, the US census office announced that the Indian Frontier had ended: nowhere within the USA's borders now belonged to the Plains Indians (see page 96).

Figure: Events leading to the Wounded Knee Massacre.

Extend your knowledge

American Indian legacy

It would be wrong to see the American Indian peoples of America as having been defeated forever. Through the 20th century, American Indians fought for their civil rights. The Massacre at Wounded Knee became a symbol of their oppression.

Exam-style question, Section A

Write a narrative account analysing the conflict between the Plains Indians and the US government in the years 1876–90.

You may use the following in your answer:

- The Battle of the Little Bighorn (1876)
- The Ghost Dance (1890).

You **must** also use information of your own. **8 marks**

Exam tip

Start by adding at least one more dated event to the list : for example, the Wounded Knee Massacre (December, 1890). You then need to describe the sequence of events in the right order, and show how one event linked to the next.

Summary

- Conflicts over land continued to cause problems of law and order, especially range wars between big cattle ranchers and other land users.
- However, in most parts of the West the government had much greater control over law and order than before, as populations increased and communications improved.
- The Johnson County War was a range war that used extreme vigilante justice – but local people refused to allow it.
- The shock of a Plains Indian victory at the Battle of the Little Bighorn made white Americans determined to remove any threat of Plains Indian resistance to white America.

Checkpoint

Strengthen

S1 Identify the key events of the Johnson County War, with the dates when they happened.

S2 Explain how the Ghost Dance was connected to the Wounded Creek Massacre.

Challenge

C1 Which of the following do you think did the most to cause conflict on the Plains: the railroads, homesteaders or gold prospecting? Back up your choice with evidence.

How confident do you feel about your answers? If you're not sure you answered them well, try working on them in a group. Divide up the tasks, so you can focus on investigating one aspect in depth before reporting back.

3.3 The destruction of the Plains Indians' way of life

The hunting and extermination* of the buffalo

In the 1860s there had been at least 25 million buffalo on the Great Plains. By 1883 they had all gone. This was because of hunting by white Americans. The US government encouraged the hunting as a way of getting Plains Indians under control.

Economic reasons for the extermination

- Before the 1870s, buffalo had been hunted for their warm coats, which were made into clothing. In 1871, a process for cheaply turning buffalo hide (skin) into the right sort of leather for the belts used in machinery was discovered. High prices for buffalo hides meant people rushed to kill as many buffalo as they could.
- Railroads brought hunters to the Plains and transported the hides back to the cities. Buffalo could be killed quickly using powerful rifles. Many hunters killed more buffalo than they were able to skin.

Once the skin was removed, the rest of the buffalo was then left to rot on the Plains.

Extermination south and north

- In 1872–74 professional buffalo hunters killed around four and a half million buffalo in the southern half of the Great Plains. Plains Indians killed around a million buffalo during this period.
- Buffalo herds in the north of the Great Plains were protected by the Great Sioux reservation until 1876. Then the government started to break up the Sioux's control of this area. 1876 was also when the Northern Pacific Railroad reached Sioux lands.
- In 1880, an estimated 5,000 white Americans were killing and skinning buffalo in the north. By 1883, the buffalo in the north were gone.

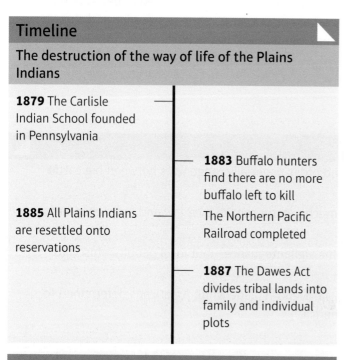

Timeline

The destruction of the way of life of the Plains Indians

1879 The Carlisle Indian School founded in Pennsylvania

1883 Buffalo hunters find there are no more buffalo left to kill

The Northern Pacific Railroad completed

1885 All Plains Indians are resettled onto reservations

1887 The Dawes Act divides tribal lands into family and individual plots

Source A

An old buffalo hunter, Frank Mayer, recalls a conversation with an Army officer that he had in the 1870s.

```
Mayer, there's no two ways about it, either
the buffalo or the Indian must go. Only when
the Indian becomes absolutely dependent on us
for his every need, will we be able to handle
him. He's too independent with the buffalo.
But if we kill the buffalo we conquer the
Indian. It seems a more humane thing to kill
the buffalo than the Indian, so the buffalo
must go.
```

Key term

Extermination*

To kill a whole population.

Extermination and government policy

Exterminating the buffalo seemed to fit in well with the US government's policy of moving Plains Indians onto reservations and encouraging them to learn farming. See Source B and the labels around it, which explain why the US government allowed the extermination of the buffalo herds.

Source B

This huge pile of buffalo skulls was photographed in the 1880s in Detroit on the way to a factory that produced fertiliser and pigment from buffalo bones.

As long as there were buffalo herds to hunt, Plains Indians resisted moving to reservations.

Some treaties had allowed tribes the right to use hunting areas outside their reservation. Once the buffalo were all killed, these rights ended, too.

As long as there were buffalo herds to hunt, Plains Indians did not need to settle down and learn farming.

As long as there were buffalo, Plains Indians were independent. Without the buffalo, many tribes needed help with food: the government used this to control them.

Impact on the Plains Indians

The loss of the buffalo destroyed the Plains Indians' way of life. Some turned to cattle ranching or farming crops. But the cattle herds were badly affected by disease and the crops failed year after year. Reservation Indians became dependent on the government for food handouts. The government reduced the food handouts to punish Plains Indians who took part in resistance. This resulted in starvation on the reservations. Lack of food lowered the Plains Indians' resistance to diseases like flu and measles, and many died.

Activities ?

1 Describe three differences between the way Plains Indians and white Americans used the buffalo.

2 Describe two consequences of the extermination of the buffalo for the Plains Indians.

3 Explain why the US government did not stop the extermination of the buffalo herds.

The Plains Indians' life on the reservations

By the 1880s, white Americans generally agreed that allowing Plains Indians to keep large reservations meant they would try to cling on to their old ways of life. The government decided to gradually get rid of reservations and push Plains Indians into assimilating* into the American way of life.

Shrinking reservations

In 1889, Indians were again pressured into accepting further reductions in reservation size. This followed the Dawes Act (1887), (see page 95). Six small Sioux reservations were created. The rest of the land from the old reservation was sold.

Taking away the power of the tribal chiefs

In the early 1880s, the US government set up special councils among the tribes. These councils were to take over from chiefs, who had often resisted further loss of land. Councils were much easier for the US government to deal with. The US negotiators were easily able to influence council members through threats and bribes. In 1883 and 1885, the powers of chiefs to judge and punish members of their tribe were taken away from them. Instead, after 1885 it was the US federal law courts that did this. This was important because it meant Plains Indians had lost all ability to govern themselves.

> **Key terms**
>
> **Assimilating***
>
> To become part of a culture or way of life.
>
> **Prejudice***
>
> When people dislike or disapprove of others because they are different, e.g. of a different race.

Government agents

Government agents used bribes of food or medical supplies to make Plains Indians do what they wanted. A number of Plains Indians joined the Indian Agency Police, where they were fed, clothed and sheltered. These Plains Indians were responsible for keeping order amongst their former tribespeople. The Indian Agency Police did what the US government ordered.

Education and religion

Plains Indian boys and girls were sent to schools outside of the reservations. If their parents resisted or refused, their food rations were withdrawn until they agreed. Once in school, the children were:

- taught not to respect the traditional way of life of their tribe
- taught to be Christians
- punished if they spoke their own language or danced their tribe's dances.

By 1887, 2,020 Plains Indian children were pupils at 117 boarding schools and 2,500 were in 110 day schools.

However, Plains Indians who had been educated as Americans still faced prejudice* from other Americans, as Source C describes.

> **Source C**
>
> Plenty Horses, a Brulé Sioux, was a pupil at Carlisle Indian School in Pennsylvania between 1883 and 1888, starting when he was 14. He gave the following account of his education to a reporter after he was put on trial for the murder of a US Army officer in 1891.
>
> I found that the education I had received was of no benefit to me. There was no chance to get employment, nothing for me to do whereby I could earn my board and clothes, no opportunities to learn more and remain with the whites. It disheartened me and I went back to live as I had before going to school.

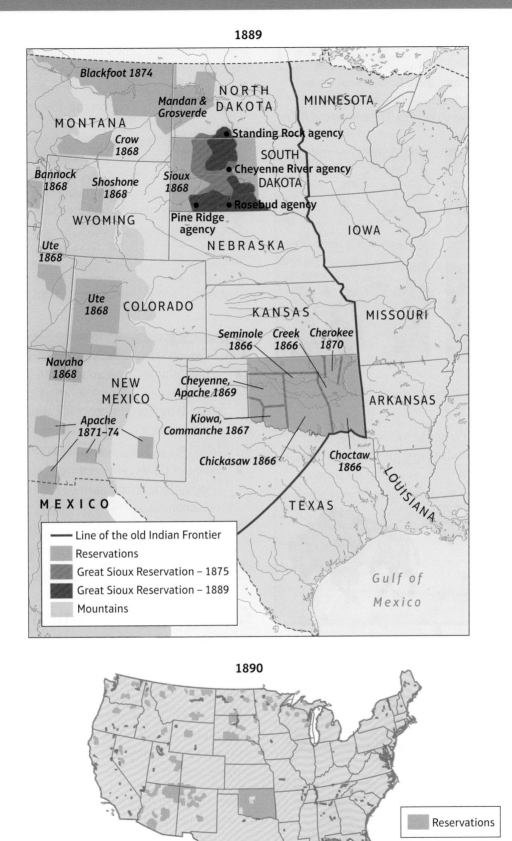

Figure 3.7 Reservations got smaller and were increasingly broken up after 1889. The top map shows the reservations for a central area of the USA in 1889 and in particular the change in size of the Great Sioux Reservation between 1875 and 1889. The bottom map shows the situation in 1890 across the whole of the USA.

Source D

Two photographs of the same three Lakota Sioux boys. The one on the left was taken when they arrived at Carlisle Indian School in Pennsylvania in 1879. The one on the right was taken six months later.

Living conditions

Exterminating the buffalo herds and reducing the reservation size had serious consequences for living conditions on the reservations, as the figure shows.

Without buffalo to hunt, the Plains Indians did not have food or the resources for making clothes or shelters.

Tribes that farmed crops struggled to grow enough to eat on the poor land of the reservations. Pests, droughts and plant diseases also made it difficult to grow enough food for everyone to live on.

Plains Indians had to rely more and more on the government for food and clothing. Disease, alcoholism and depression spread through the reservations.

Figure: How the Plains Indians' way of life changed.

Despite the social problems created by reservations, the government continued to believe that breaking up Plains Indian society would eventually mean the Plains Indians stopped relying on the government.

Source E

In 1882, Chief Sitting Bull gave an interview to a journalist while he and his family were being held at Fort Randall. As part of this interview, he said the following.

```
The life my people want is a life of freedom.
I have seen nothing that a white man has,
houses or railways or clothing or food, that
is as good as the right to move in the open
country, and live in our fashion.
```

Activities ?

1 Using Source C and Source D to help you, write a diary account for one of the Lakota boys, describing how different life was at the Carlisle Indian School compared to their life amongst the Lakota.

2 How did US government policy towards reservations change after 1876? Describe at least two changes.

3 Explain why white Americans did not agree with Sitting Bull (Source E) about what was best for his people.

Changing government attitudes to the Plains Indians

From 1834, US government policy was to move Plains Indians to reservations in order to keep them away from white settlers. The reservations had been set up and were protected by US law through treaties. The treaties were signed by chiefs, as representatives of the Plains Indian tribes.

However, as you have seen, this policy changed dramatically over time.

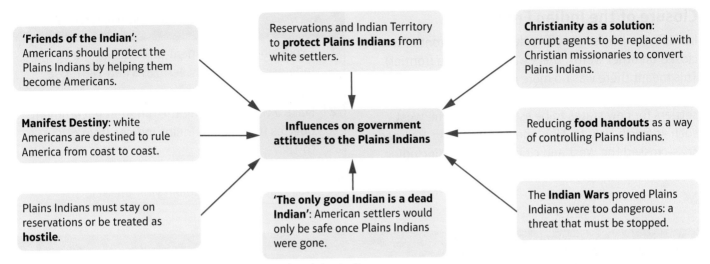

Figure 3.8 Influences on government attitudes to the Plains Indians.

By the late 1880s, much had changed.

- The Plains Indians' way of life had been destroyed.
- Chiefs had lost their powers to lead and protect their people.
- Plains Indian children were not taught their tribes' traditions or way of life.

The US government thought the changes would force the Plains Indians to learn farming and become like other US citizens. But instead, most seemed to sink into poverty and sickness, surviving on government handouts.

The government decided that the reservation system was causing the problem.

- Although the chiefs had no political power, their people still looked up to them. The chiefs wanted to return to the traditional way of life and resisted further changes.
- The tribes shared work and food between them instead of competing against each other to have the most land or money, as white Americans did.

The Dawes Act (1887)

The Dawes Act of 1887 was like a Homestead Act for Plains Indians. Each Plains Indian family was allotted a 160-acre share of reservation land. Plains Indians who took up the offer could then become American citizens. The Act was only passed in Congress once something else was added to it: all the reservation land left over could be sold to whites. This land was often bought by railroad companies and land speculators.

The aims of the Dawes Act were to:

- break up the power of the tribe and encourage individualism
- encourage individual families to farm for themselves, rather than relying on the tribe
- encourage Plains Indians to give up their traditional way of life and become American citizens
- free up more land for white settlers
- reduce the cost to the federal government of running the reservation system.

Significance of the Dawes Act

The result of the Dawes Act was that, by 1890, Plains Indians had lost half the lands they had in 1887.

- Those who took up the offered land found it impossible to make a living farming. Most gave up and sold their land to white settlers.
- Those who kept land passed it on to their children, dividing the land up into smaller plots. These smaller plots made farming even harder.
- Many Plains Indians were cheated out of their land by white settlers.

As a result, life for Plains Indians became even harder. However, white settlers benefited by getting hold of more land.

Closure of the Indian Frontier

In 1890, the US census office declared the Frontier was closed (in other words, there was no longer a frontier). This meant there was no more land in the USA that white Americans did not control. There were enough settlers for new states to be established in the West, such as North Dakota, Montana and Wyoming. Railroads criss-crossed the West and cities had grown, including mining towns and cow towns.

Activities ?

1   Explain how government attitudes to the Plains Indians changed between 1876 and 1887. Use Figure 3.8 to help you

2   Make a timeline listing the different government policies towards the Plains Indians from c1834 to 1887.

3   What did the Dawes Act (1887) aim to achieve? Was is successful? Explain your answer.

Summary

- The US government policy to keep Plains Indians away from white Americans on reservations was strengthened by the extermination of the buffalo. The government did nothing to stop this.

- Reservation life was very tough and, by the 1880s, many US government officials thought the Plains Indians could only be 'saved' if the reservation system was ended.

- The Dawes Act of 1887 did not achieve its aims of encouraging Plains Indians to become independent homesteaders and American citizens. By the time the Frontier was closed in 1890, Plains Indians had lost half the land they had in 1887.

Checkpoint

Strengthen

S1   Explain the importance of the buffalo to the Plains Indians.

S2   Describe the ways the US government used politics, food, religion and education to control Plains Indians on reservations.

Challenge

C1   Explain three consequences of the Dawes Act for the way of life of the Plains Indians.

How confident do you feel about your answers? If you are not sure you answered these questions well, go back to the text in this section to find the details you need.

Recall quiz

1   When was the terrible winter that meant the end of the open range?
2   Who was the leader of the 7th Cavalry when they were defeated by Crazy Horse in 1876?
3   What was the name given to the religious cult of the 1890s that looked to the Great Spirit to restore the Plains Indians' way of life to them?
4   In what year did hunters realise that there were no more buffalo to hunt?
5   In 1892, a range war broke out in which county of Wyoming?
6   The Sioux called them Paha Sapa: what was the English name for the sacred hills where gold was discovered in 1874, triggering the Sioux Wars?
7   Which two ranching families were Wyatt Earp and his brothers in conflict with in Tombstone, Arizona in 1881?
8   Which state did most Exodusters migrate to?
9   Which lawman caught Billy the Kid, saw him escape and then shot him in 1881?
10 In which year did the US census office declare the Frontier was closed?

Activities

1   Continue a timeline of your American West studies. Use this chapter to note down key dates for your timeline. You should start from 1876 and end in 1895.
2   Create Snap cards for the American West: each one a key feature or key event from the period (1830s–1895). Each player places a card face up at the same time. The first person to make a valid link between the two cards wins the pair. Some example cards are shown here.

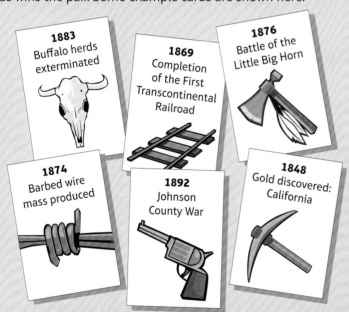

1883 Buffalo herds exterminated

1869 Completion of the First Transcontinental Railroad

1876 Battle of the Little Big Horn

1874 Barbed wire mass produced

1892 Johnson County War

1848 Gold discovered: California

3   Thinking about everything you have learned in this chapter, which one event would you argue was the most significant for the settlement of the American West in the period from 1876 to 1895? Explain the choice you have made.

Exam-style question, Section A

Explain **two** of the following:

- The importance of the Battle of the Little Bighorn (1876) for government attitudes towards the Plains Indians.
- The importance of the Johnson County War (1892) for law and order in the West.
- The importance of the Oklahoma Land Rush of 1893 for settlement of the West.

16 marks

Exam tip

This question is testing your ability to explain how and why an event is significant.

- The question asks why something is important *for something else*.
- Use this to keep your answer relevant. You could start: 'The Oklahoma Land Rush was important for settlement of the West because…'

Writing historically: narrative analysis

When you write a narrative analysis, you need to explain a series of events: their causes and consequences. You need to think about how you express the links between **causes** and **effects**.

Learning outcomes

By the end of this lesson, you will understand how to:

- use conjunctions to link and indicate the relationship between points
- use non-finite verbs to show the relationship between points.

Definitions

Co-ordinating conjunction: a word used to link two clauses of equal importance within a sentence, e.g. 'and', 'but', 'so', 'or', etc.

Subordinate clause: a clause that adds detail to or develops the main clause.

How can I link my points in sentences to show cause and effect?

When explaining a complex sequence of events, use **co-ordinating conjunctions** to link them in sentences.

1. Look at this exam-style question:

> Write a narrative account analysing the conflict between the Plains Indians and the US government in the years 1876–1890. **(8 marks)**

How could you link these three points using just 'and', 'but', 'so' (co-ordinating conjunctions)?

> In 1874, the Northern Pacific Railroad was approaching Sioux hunting grounds in Dakota.
>
> Custer used his mission of protecting the rail workers to prospect for gold in the Black Hills.
>
> Thousands of prospectors swarmed all over the Black Hills.

You can also use **subordinating** conjunctions to make the relationship between cause and effect clear. For example, linking:

- an explanation: (e.g. 'because', 'as', 'in order that', etc)
- a condition: (e.g. 'if', 'unless', etc)
- a comparison: (e.g. 'although', 'whereas', 'despite', etc)
- a sequence: (e.g. 'when', 'as', 'before', 'after', 'until', etc).

2. Look at these simple, short questions and answers:

a. Why did the government claim the Plains Indians had broken the Fort Laramie Treaty? *Government attempts to buy the land were refused and Plains Indian raids continued.*

b. What caused thousands of Plains Indians to leave their reservations? *They believed the government had betrayed them, breaking the Fort Laramie Treaty.*

c. What was the result of the government demand that the Plains Indians return? *Winter weather largely prevented them doing so, meaning that they were declared hostile.*

d. Why did Custer lose at Little Big Horn? *He was badly outnumbered and failed to wait for reinforcements.*

At the moment a, b, c and d are each made up of two sentences: a question and an answer.

Rewrite each statement and answer so that they become one whole sentence. For example:

> One reason why the government claimed the Plains Indians had broken the Fort Laramie Treaty was because government attempts to buy the land were refused and Plains Indian raids continued.

How can I link my points in other ways?

You can add relevant information and further explanation of cause and effect using **non-finite verbs**. For example: facing / faced, determining / determined, cutting / cut.

Compare these two extracts, written in response to the exam-style question on the previous page:

> The US government had to change its approach because it was faced with great public pressure after Little Big Horn.

Two points are linked using a subordinating conjunction.

> Faced with great public pressure after Little Big Horn, the US government had to change its approach.

Two points are linked using a non-finite verb.

Look at the sentence below. How could you link the two points, using a non-finite verb instead of a conjunction? **Hint:** think about how you could use a non-finite form of the highlighted verb.

> Wovoka was determined to encourage Plains Indians to resist reservation life, so he began the Ghost Dance.

Improving an answer

Now look at this paragraph from the beginning of one student's response to the exam-style narrative analysis task on the previous page:

> Sitting Bull's followers fled south to escape the army and joined Big Foot. The army caught up with them and took them to Wounded Knee Creek. A Sioux warrior resisted being disarmed and others began to dance. A shot was fired. The 7th Cavalry opened fire with repeating rifles and machine guns. 250 Sioux and 25 soldiers died.

3. Try rewriting this paragraph, using conjunctions and non-finite verbs to make the sequence of events, and the relationship between cause and effect, clear.

Writing analytical narrative

The difference between a story and a narrative account that analyses

Paper 2, Question 2 will ask you to 'Write a narrative account analysing…' (see page 102 in *Preparing for your exams*). This does not mean just writing a story. It means explaining how events are linked together in order.

To write a narrative analysis, you must:

- show how one event caused another event or made a change to something else
- show how the events in the narrative account are linked together in a sequence*.

It is the way that you link the events together that is important.

Narratives for young children are always stories. They describe what happened. For example, the book *The Wind in the Willows* has stories about Toad of Toad Hall. These narratives show how Toad got himself into a number of scrapes. One story describes his obsession with fast cars, then him stealing one, then him being arrested, and finally him being sent to prison.

Here is a short part of *The Wind in the Willows*.

Toad steals a motor car

> Toad had a passion for cars. He saw a car in the middle of the yard, quite unattended. Toad walked slowly round it. 'I wonder,' he said to himself, 'if this car starts easily.' Next moment he was turning the starting handle. Then he heard the sound of the engine and, as if in a dream, he found himself in the driver's seat. He drove the car out through the archway and the car leapt forward through the open country... .

This has the first part of a narrative: a sequence of events in the right order. The author used words and phrases like 'next moment' and 'then' to show the sequence.

So what is missing? There are no analytical links between events. The author could have used words like 'because', 'in order to' or 'as a result of this'.

For example:

> Toad saw the car parked in the middle of the yard. Because there was no one with it, he took the opportunity to have a good look at it. He even gave the starting handle a turn in order to see how easily it started. It started easily, but the sound of the engine affected Toad so much that his old passion for cars resurfaced and his urge to drive the car increased to such an extent that it became irresistible. As a result, as if in a dream, he found himself in the driver's seat...

The new linking words make it clear what difference each step made. And process words* show something was happening. In this example, the process words and phrases are 'affected', 'resurfaced', 'increased' and 'became'.

Activities ?

1. Choose a story that you know well – or make up a story of your own.

2. a. Select up to six key events in the story. Your events should be from the beginning, middle and end of the story.

   b. Create a flow chart with arrows from one event to the next in the sequence, like this.

   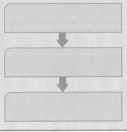

   c. Label your arrows with linking phrases* chosen from the chain of linkages (see Figure 1).

3. Write a one-paragraph narrative account analysing the key events of your story.

   - Use linking phrases.
   - Add at least **three** process words. (You can find ideas in the process word case – Figure 2 – or choose your own.)

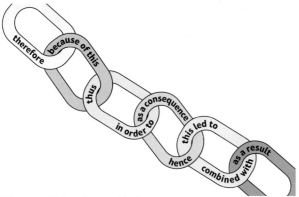

Figure 1 The chain of linkages.

Figure 2 Process word case.

Writing historical accounts analysing…

You may be asked to write an account that analyses the key events which led to something, or the key events of a crisis, or the way in which something developed. This example has shown the skills you will need to write a good historical account.

As you prepare for your examination, you should practise by:

- selecting key events
- writing them in sequence
- linking them into a process that explains an outcome*.

As you study the American West, note the linking phrases and process words the author has used in this book. When you create your own analytical historical narratives, try to make use of both linking phrases and process words.

Key terms

Sequence*

The order that events happened in.

Process words*

Words that show how an event changed things.

Linking phrases*

Words that show the links between events.

Outcome*

The result of an event or change. It can be positive or negative.

Activities ?

Study the timeline on page 49. You can use the events from it to help you to answer the following question:

Write a narrative account analysing the key events of the growth of the cattle industry, 1861–70.

1 With a partner, write the events on pieces of card, without their dates, and then:

   a sort them into the correct order, then jumble them up again and sort them into order a second time

   b decide on two or three key events that you could include in your account and remove any events you don't need to include.

2 Working on your own, write a one-paragraph narrative account. Focus on what it is you are explaining – the growth of the cattle industry. Choose process words which relate to growth, e.g. 'extended', 'expanded' and 'created'.

3 Either swap accounts with a partner or check your own account.

   a Highlight linking phrases in yellow.

   b Highlight process words in green.

   c Can you find a way to add one more linking phrase or process word to the paragraph?

You are now ready to complete your exam question. Remember to use **SSLaP**.

- **S**elect key events and developments.
- **S**equence them in the right order.
- **L**ink them, **and**
- Use **P**rocess words to show what had changed in the outcome.

Preparing for your GCSE Paper 2 exam

Paper 2 overview

Paper 2 has two sections. Section A will be your questions on The American West, c1835–c1895 (your Period Study). These questions are worth 20% of your GCSE History assessment. The whole exam is 1 hour 45 minutes. You should use 50 minutes to do Section A. That will leave time for Section B, which is your British Depth Study.

History Paper 2	Period Study and British Depth Study			Time 1 hour 45 mins
Section A	Period Study	Answer 3 questions	32 marks	50 minutes
Section B	Depth Options B1 or B2	Answer 3 questions	32 marks	55 minutes

Period Study Option 24/25: The American West, c1835–c1895

You will answer Questions 1, 2 and 3.

1 Explain two consequences of... (2 x 4 marks)

- Time – 10 minutes.
- What – explain two consequences.
- Length – up to half a page on each consequence.
- Focus – on the consequence or outcomes.
- Helpful phrases – 'as a result', 'as a consequence', 'the effect was'.
- Hints – keep it brief. Don't add extra information on extra lines.

2 Write a narrative account analysing... (8 marks)

- Time – 15 minutes.
- What – a narrative analysis that links events and shows how they led to an outcome. The question will have two hint bullet points.
- Length – up to two pages, but you do not have to use all the space.
- Focus – on linking events together to explain an outcome.
- Helpful phrases – the linking phrases and process words on page 101.
- Hints – focus on getting the events in the right order. It should have a beginning, middle and end.

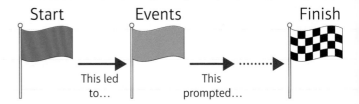

3 Explain the importance of two... (2 x 8 marks)

- Time – 25 minutes.
- What – an explanation of how an event was important.
- Length – one page per event.
- Focus – showing how the event was important, or in other words, 'What difference did it make?'
- Helpful phrases – 'this caused', 'this led to', 'this was important because'.
- Hints – remember that you pick two out of the three options to answer. Make sure that your reason for saying it is important is clear.

Paper 2, Question 1

Explain **two** consequences of the introduction of barbed wire in the West (1874). (**8 marks**)

Exam tip

The question wants you to explain the results of something. What difference did it make? Use phrases such as 'as a result' or 'the effect of this was'.

Basic answer

Consequence 1:
Barbed wire was invented in 1874 by Joseph F. Glidden, who improved on an earlier idea for using wire instead of wood for fences. Because barbed wire has spikes on it cattle stay away from it, but there was conflict between homesteaders and cattlemen as a result of using barbed wire.

This general information about barbed wire is correct but it is not being used to explain consequences. Saying that barbed wire led to the conflict is too vague.

Consequence 2:
Barbed wire was also used by homesteaders to fence in their plots. They needed fences to keep their own livestock off their crops and also to keep other people's livestock off their crops. The consequence was that it made farming easier.

This is correct but, again, too general and vague. We need to know what difference the introduction of barbed wire made – the consequence of it being introduced. For example, what fencing difficulties did it solve?

Verdict

This is a basic answer because it identifies two consequences with some support, but it needs more explanation of consequences with specific information.
Use the feedback to rewrite this answer, making as many improvements as you can.

Paper 2, Question 1

Explain **two** consequences of the introduction of barbed wire in the West (1874). (**8 marks**)

Exam tip

The question wants you to explain the results of something. What difference did it make? Use phrases such as 'as a result' or 'the effect of this was'.

Good answer

Consequence 1:
The use of barbed wire by homesteaders caused problems for cattle ranchers. Because homesteaders' claims usually included a water source, fences often prevented cattlemen's cows from reaching water. Sometimes, cattlemen cut the barbed wire to let their cattle through. The cattle might then eat the homesteaders' crops. So a consequence of barbed wire was conflict between homesteaders and cattle ranchers.

Consequence 2:
Timber for fencing was very expensive, but homesteaders needed to fence off their crops to protect them from animals. A consequence of barbed wire was that it solved this problem of a lack of timber on the Plains. Large areas of land could be fenced off cheaply.

This answer explains why barbed wire led to conflict between cattle ranchers and homesteaders. It uses details from the student's knowledge to back the answer up.

Good use of detail that is specific to the period and relevant to the question. Setting out the problem before the introduction of barbed wire has made the consequence much easier to explain.

Verdict

This is a good answer because two clear consequences are now provided, and are backed up by relevant, specific information.

Paper 2, Question 2

Write a narrative account analysing the key events in the years 1851–66 that led to the beginning of Red Cloud's War. You may use the following in your answer:

- the Fort Laramie Treaty (1851)
- the discovery of gold in Montana.

You **must** also use information of your own. **(8 marks)**

Exam tip

Remember that the key to scoring well on this type of question is to explain how one event leads to the next in a logical and structured way.

Basic answer

Red Cloud's War began in 1866 after the US Army began building forts in lands that had been granted to the Sioux by the Fort Laramie Treaty.

This introduction to the answer uses accurate information but could be improved by starting at the beginning of the narrative account, not the end, e.g. 'The Fort Laramie Treaty of 1851 granted lands to the Sioux…'

The forts were built by the US Army to protect prospectors travelling across Sioux hunting lands to Montana. The government had ordered the army to protect the travellers, even though they were breaking the Fort Laramie Treaty. This caused Red Cloud's War.

Instead of writing about causes of the war, the student should have identified key events leading up to the war and analysed the ways these events linked together to produce an outcome: the beginning of war.

The most important cause of Red Cloud's War was the discovery of gold in Montana. Prospectors began to travel across the Sioux's hunting grounds. The Sioux attacked the white Americans and the US government sent in the army to protect the travellers. When the army started to build forts, the war began.

The student has listed some key events here and started to look at the links between them, but not in enough depth and still with the aim of identifying causes, which is not the right approach here.

Verdict

This is a basic answer because:

- the student should have identified key events leading up to the war, but did not do this well enough
- these events should have been set out in a logical order (the order in which they happened is usually the best approach) and the student should have considered the ways in which one event related to the next. This did not happen enough in this answer.

Use the feedback to rewrite this answer, making as many improvements as you can.

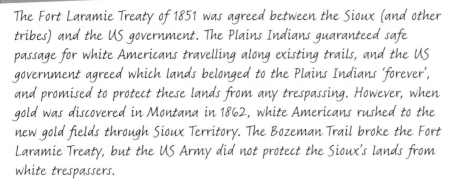

Paper 2, Question 2

Write a narrative account analysing the key events in the years 1851–66 that led to the beginning of Red Cloud's War. **(8 marks)**

Good answer

The Fort Laramie Treaty of 1851 was agreed between the Sioux (and other tribes) and the US government. The Plains Indians guaranteed safe passage for white Americans travelling along existing trails, and the US government agreed which lands belonged to the Plains Indians 'forever', and promised to protect these lands from any trespassing. However, when gold was discovered in Montana in 1862, white Americans rushed to the new gold fields through Sioux Territory. The Bozeman Trail broke the Fort Laramie Treaty, but the US Army did not protect the Sioux's lands from white trespassers.

> The student has identified the first events in their narrative. Giving accurate dates for events helps structure the narrative.

As a result furious Sioux warriors attacked the travellers. This led to the US government saying that the Plains Indians had broken the treaty, too.

The US government organised a peace council in 1866. The government negotiators wanted white settlers to be allowed safe passage along the Bozeman Trail, and for new forts to be built along the trail to 'protect' Plains Indian lands. Red Cloud refused to allow the Bozeman Trail or the forts.

> Links are made between key events, e.g. the Bozeman Trail broke the Fort Laramie Treaty, and the consequences that followed from this. This is shown by phrases like 'As a result'.

Red Cloud learned that soldiers had started bringing in materials to build forts anyway. As a consequence, Red Cloud left the council, certain that the Sioux must defend their lands by force. Red Cloud's War then began.

> The student has included some linking phrases like 'as a consequence', but more could be added to improve the answer.

Verdict

This is a good answer because:
- key events are identified
- these events are structured in a logical order
- the student has added some analysis of how the events linked together to produce the outcome – Red Cloud's War.

The answer could be improved further by adding some more analysis, for example, of why negotiations between the Sioux and the government broke down.

Paper 2, Question 3

Explain **two** of the following:
- The importance of cattle trails for the development of the cattle industry in the 1860s.
- The importance of the railroads for changes in the way of life of the Plains Indians.
- The importance of the wagon trails for the early settlement of the West. **(16 marks)**

Exam tip

In the exam, you will have two separate answer sheets in the booklet for this question, one for each of the two answers you give in Question 3. Make sure you indicate at the start of each answer which point you are addressing: you are prompted to do this.

Basic answer

Cattle trails: In the Civil War, in the years 1861-65, the longhorn herds of cattle increased in Texas and they were not worth much money. After the Civil War, there was high demand for beef in the northern cities. Goodnight and Loving made the first Long Drive after the Civil War to Fort Sumner.

Cattle trails were very important to the cattle industry because cowboys herded large herds of cattle up the trails from Texas to the railheads in Kansas and Missouri.

The student uses relevant points to describe the use of cattle trails. However, the student is not explaining *how* the cattle trails were important for the development of the cattle industry.

Railroads: The railroads were important because now the USA was connected from east to west. The cattle industry also developed because of railroads, with cow towns like Abilene growing up at railheads. All this meant more whites travelling across the Plains and that was not good for the Plains Indians.

The point is correct, but needs more explanation of the impact on the way of life of the Plains Indians – why was it 'not good' for the Plains Indians?.

The railroad also brought products from big cities to settlers on the Plains, such as farm machinery and barbed wire. The railroads also took the farmers' crops back to the cities so they could be sold.

The railroad was very bad for the Plains Indians because it meant that all the buffalo were killed. The trains brought hunters to the Plains.

These two paragraphs include good details about the importance of railroads, but the question is about their importance for the way of life of the Plains Indians and this has not been explained.

Verdict

This is a basic answer because of the following points.
- More development is needed: the student needs to focus their answer on *explaining* importance. For example, 'The cattle trails helped the development of the cattle industry *because*…'.
- In the second answer, the student does not connect points to importance for changes in the way of life of the Plains Indians. This could be done, for example, by adding '…and that was not good for the Plains Indians *because*…'.

Use the feedback to rewrite this answer, making as many improvements as you can.

Paper 2, Question 3

Explain **two** of the following:

- The importance of cattle trails for the development of the cattle industry in the 1860s.
- The importance of the railroads for changes in the way of life of the Plains Indians.
- The importance of the wagon trails for the early settlement of the West.

(16 marks)

Only one development is demonstrated below but your answer in the exam will have to explain a **second** choice as well.

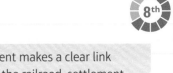

Good answer

Railroads

The railroads encouraged people to come and live in the West. For example, the 1862 Pacific Railroad Act meant railroad companies were given huge areas of land alongside railroad tracks to sell to new settlers. These settlers came to live in areas where Plains Indians lived and hunted. Settlers were worried about Plains Indians attacking them or stealing from them. They wanted the US government to move Plains Indians to reservations and the US government did this.

The student makes a clear link between the railroad, settlement and pressure on Plains Indians to move to reservations. The student also uses relevant evidence about the Pacific Railroad Act to support their answer. The student could improve their answer by giving more specific information about how the Plains Indians' way of life was changed as a result of settlement.

Another way the railroads caused changes for the Plains Indians was because, in the 1870s, the railroads brought professional white American hunters to the Plains, who killed buffalo for their skins and then could use the railroads to transport the hides back to the cities. As a result, the hunters exterminated the buffalo herds. Plains Indians needed buffalo for food, clothing and shelter. Their way of life was all about following buffalo herds so that wasn't possible either any more. Their lives changed because they now had to rely on government handouts of food, and on farming instead of hunting.

The student's link between the railroads and the extermination of the buffalo herds makes a convincing reason for why the railroads were important in changing the way of life of the Plains Indians. One sentence – 'so that wasn't possible either any more' – isn't as clear as it could be. The answer could be further improved by more specific information, for example about the numbers of buffalo killed.

Verdict

This is a good answer because:

- it shows a clear understanding of the period
- the student analyses ways in which the railroads were important in changes to the lives of the Plains Indians.

Answers to Recall Quiz questions

Chapter 1

1 Any three reasonable answers, e.g. for food, hide used to make clothes, fur used to make blankets

2 Mexico

3 Problems included: lack of timber to build houses with; lack of timber to build fences with; lack of wood to burn for fuel

4 1851

5 A financial crisis, and it led to a long-lasting economic depression in the USA

6 Bad decisions included: setting off late (May 1846, when April would have given them more time); the decision of the 80 migrants to try the new route; believing that the trail guide had actually completed this short cut; arguing amongst themselves about which route to take; not turning back when the short cut proved to be much more difficult than expected; deciding to tackle the Sierra Nevada mountains in late October – too late to be safe

7 Three reasons could include: a central plan was developed that worked out the details of what everyone needed to do; the Mormons' religious beliefs meant that everyone followed the plan rather than wasting time arguing over what to do for the best; the Mormons were able to use irrigation in the area from streams feeding into the Great Salt Lake; the Mormons

spread their settlements over a wide area and then made each settlement specialise in something that all Mormons would benefit from; the Mormon pioneers were soon joined by large numbers of new Mormon migrants who all helped to build the settlements; Mormons around the world gave money to the settlements; Mormons believed that God was helping them build settlements in the desert, which improved their morale and ability to withstand suffering and difficulties

8 False, although it did create the idea of areas of land 'belonging' to each tribe, which was a first step towards reservations

9 The belief that white Americans had the right to populate all areas of America from East Coast to West Coast

10 To keep Plains Indians and white Americans apart

Chapter 2

1 The American Civil War ended in 1865 with the North (or Union) winning the war

2 160 acres

3 The Union Pacific and the Central Pacific

4 1869

5 Barbed wire

6 Chisholm Trail

7 John Iliff

8 Your answer could include one of the following: filing claims

under the Homestead Act for the bits of land on the ranch which contained waterholes or springs; ranch-hands and family members would file Homestead Act claims to parcels of land throughout the ranch area and then hand those rights over to the ranch; by taking homesteaders to court over claims, knowing that most homesteaders did not have the money to pay lawyers and court costs and so would have to give up their claims; by threatening homesteaders with violence, damaging their crops and accusing them of rustling cows from the ranch's herd, which could end up in severe punishments for the homesteader

9 The Bozeman Trail

10 President Ulysses S. Grant

Chapter 3

1 The winter began in 1886 and ended in 1887, so it's usually known as the winter of 1886–87

2 Custer: Lieutenant Colonel George Armstrong Custer

3 The Ghost Dance

4 1883

5 Johnson County

6 The Black Hills

7 The Clantons and the McLaurys

8 Kansas

9 Pat Garrett

10 1890

Index

Key terms are capitalized initially, in bold type with an asterisk.
Headings for topic booklets are shown in italics.

Acknowledgements

P14 Cengage Learning: The Cheyennes: Indians of the Great Plains (Case Studies in Cultural Anthropology), 6 Mar. 1978. **P15 U.S Government:** The US government policy towards the Plains Indians. **p22 Captain Fellun:** Captain Fellun, who led one of the rescue parties, described what he found when he reached the Donner Party in February 1847. **P23 Lansford Warren Hastings:** A description of Salt Lake Valley, written by one of the first settlers. **P27 Crowell-Collier Publishing Company:** The Plains Indians (1976) by F. Haines. **P40 Valerie Weeks Scott:** Univ Of Montana/ Bureau Of Business & Economic Res. **P53 The Cincinnati Enquirer:** The Denver Times, 'The Cattle King of Colorado', 23 February 1878. **P53 Oxford University Press:** The Great American Desert (1966) by W. E. Hollon. **P61 eHistory:** http://invasionofamerica.ehistory.org/ . **p62 Ulysses S.Grant:** President Grant's State of the Union speech, 6 December 1869. **P63 Little Crow:** Little Crow, Spokesman for the Sioux, by Gary Clayton Anderson. **P66 United States Senate:** Treaty of Fort Laramie (1868). **P4 Oxford University Press:** The Great American Desert (1966) by W. E. Hollon. **P87 Chicago Tribune:** Chicago Tribune, 7 July 1876. **P90 Sage Books:** 1 Frank H. Mayer and Charles B. Roth, The Buffalo Harvest (Denver, 1958), 29-30. **P94 Sitting Bull:** In 1882, Chief Sitting Bull interview James Creelman. On the Great Highway. The Wanderings and Adventures of a Special Correspondent. Boston: Lothrop Publishing Co., 1901. 299-302.

Photographs

(Key: t-top; b-bottom; c-centre; l-left; r-right)

Cover: The Bridgeman Art Library Ltd/Barry, David Frances (1854-1934)/ Private Collection.

The Bridgeman Art Library Ltd: Jackson, William Henry (1843-1942)/ Private Collection/Peter Newark American Pictures 6, 23, **AKG IMAGES LTD:** lam 8, 20, **Alamy:** World History Archive 4, 47, Nawrocki/ClassicStock 7cl, 44, Granger, Nyc 7cr, 32, 50, 62, 65, 73, 79, 84, North Wind Picture Archives 10l, 38, 55, 64, Interfoto 10c, 56, JT Vintage/Glasshouse Images 10r, Everett Collection Historical 29, Wendy White 81, robertharding 87, Niday Picture Library 88, Joe King 91, **Library of Congress:** 33, **Duke University Libraries:** 41, **Getty images:** Archive Photos/Stringer 12, Hulton Archive/Stringer 24, Universal History Archive 25, Bettmann 43, Dea Picture Library/De Agostini Picture Library 59, Mpi/Stringer/Archive Photos 70, Fotosearch 76, ullstein bild 94l, 94r, **TopFoto:** The Granger Collection 77.